ROTHERHAM LIBRARY & INFORMATION SERVICES

This book must be returned by the date specified at the time of issue
as the DATE DUE FOR RETURN.
The loan may be extended (personally, by post or telephone) for a
further period if the book is not required by another reader, by quoting
the above number / author / title.

LIS7a

Match of My Life

SHEFFIELD UTD

KNOW THE SCORE BOOKS PUBLICATIONS

CULT HEROES	Author	ISBN
CHELSEA	Leo Moynihan	1-905449-00-3
NEWCASTLE	Dylan Younger	1-905449-03-8
SOUTHAMPTON	Jeremy Wilson	1-905449-01-1
WEST BROM	Simon Wright	1-905449-02-X

MATCH OF MY LIFE	Editor	ISBN
ENGLAND WORLD CUP	Massarella & Moynihan	1-905449-52-6
EUROPEAN CUP FINALS	Ben Lyttleton	1-905449-57-7
FA CUP FINALS (1953-1969)	David Saffer	1-905449-53-4
FULHAM	Michael Heatley	1-905449-51-8
LEEDS	David Saffer	1-905449-54-2
LIVERPOOL	Leo Moynihan	1-905449-50-X
SHEFFIELD UNITED	Nick Johnson	1-905449-62-3
STOKE CITY	Simon Lowe	1-905449-55-0
SUNDERLAND	Rob Mason	1-905449-60-7
SPURS	Allen & Massarella	1-905449-58-5
WOLVES	Simon Lowe	1-905449-56-9

HARRY HARRIS	Author	ISBN
WORLD CUP DIARY	Harry Harris	1-905449-90-9
HOLD THE BACK PAGE	Harry Harris	1-905449-91-7

AUTOBIOGRAPHY	Author	ISBN
TACKLES LIKE A FERRET (England Cover)	Paul Parker	1-905449-47-X
TACKLES LIKE A FERRET (Manchester United Cover)	Paul Parker	1-905449-46-1

FOOTBALL FICTION	Author	ISBN
BURKSEY The Autobiography of a Football God	Peter Morfoot	1-905449-49-6

CRICKET	Author	ISBN
MOML: THE ASHES	Pilger & Wightman	1-905449-63-1

FORTHCOMING PUBLICATIONS IN 2007

CULT HEROES	Author	ISBN
CELTIC	David Potter	978-1-905449-08-8
DERBY	David McVay	978-1-905449-06-4
MANCHESTER CITY	David Clayton	978-1-905449-05-7
RANGERS	Paul Smith	978-1-905449-07-1

MATCH OF MY LIFE	Editor	ISBN
BOLTON WANDERERS	David Saffer	978-1-905449-64-4
FA CUP FINALS (1970-1989)	David Saffer	978-1-905449-65-1
MANCHESTER UNITED	Sam Pilger	978-1-905449-59-0
NOTTINGHAM FOREST	Grahame Lloyd	978-1-905449-66-8

GENERAL FOOTBALL	Author	ISBN
OUTCASTS The Lands FIFA Forgot	Steve Menary	978-1-905449-31-6
PARISH TO PLANET A History of Football	Dr Eric Midwinter	978-1-905449-30-9
MY PREMIERSHIP DIARY Reading's Season in the Premiership	Marcus Hahnemann	978-1-905449-33-0

CRICKET	Author	ISBN
THE 2006/7 ASHES IN PICTURES	Andrew Searle	978-1-905449-44-6
GROVEL! The 1976 West IndiesTour of England	David Tossell	978-1-905449-43-9
MY AUTOBIOGRAPHY	Shaun Udal	978-1-905449-42-2
SMILE LIKE U MEAN IT	Paul Smith	978-1-905449-45-3

Match of My Life

SHEFFIELD UTD

Editor: Nick Johnson

Series Editor: Simon Lowe
Know The Score Books Limited

www.knowthescorebooks.com

First published in the United Kingdom
by Know The Score Books Limited, 2006

The right of Nick Johnson to be identified as the author of this work has been asserted by him in accordance with sections 77 and 78 of the Copyright, Designs and Patents Act, 1988.

Know The Score Books Limited
118 Alcester Road
Studley
Warwickshire
B80 7NT

www.knowthescorebooks.com

A CIP catalogue record is available for this book from the British Library
ISBN-10: 1-905449-62-3   ISBN-13: 978-1-905449-62-0

Jacket and book design by Lisa David
Printed and bound in Great Britain
By Cromwell Press, Trowbridge, Wiltshire

Front cover:
Top Left Keith Edwards' two Golden Boots from his goalscoring exploits at Bramall Lane reside in the United Hall of Fame
Bottom Left David Unsworth celebrates the late winner against Hull which signalled United's promotion to the Premiership in 2006, Phil Jagielka's chosen match
Bottom Right Tony Currie was the hub of the exciting United team during the Golden Era of the late Sixties and early Seventies
Rear cover:
Top Left Dave Bassett celebrates promotion in 1990 by kissing striker Tony Agana
Top Right Alan Kelly is chaired from the pitch after Second Division United reach the FA Cup semi-final thanks to his saves in a penalty shoot-out against Premiership Coventry
Bottom Modern Blades legend Phil Jagielka led United back into the big time in 2006

Editor's Acknowledgements

It would not have been possible to write this book without the co-operation of the players, past and present, who kindly agreed to be interviewed. I would therefore like to take this opportunity to thank all the interviewees for sparing the time to talk to me and sharing some wonderful memories from their time at Bramall Lane.

I am also grateful to publisher Simon Lowe for inviting me to write this book. Simon's patience and understanding was much appreciated when the deadline had to be extended following unforseen delays in arranging the final interviews. I think it was worth the wait to be able to speak to some of United's greatest legends about their favourite matches.

'I would like to thank Andy Pack and John Garrett at Sheffield United, along with photographer Mark Rodgers. Thanks also go to long-standing Blades fan Terry Maguire for the loan of various books and programmes.

I also wish to acknowledge the help of staff in the local studies department at Sheffield Central Library as I conducted my research. I was further aided by referring to *A Complete Record of Sheffield United Football Club*, an excellent book written by Denis Clarebrough and Andrew Kirkham.

Finally, a big thank you to the legendary Derek Dooley for writing the foreword. 'Legend' is an overused word in football, but the term is entirely appropriate in Derek's case and I was delighted when he readily accepted my invitation.

Nick Johnson
September 2006

Contents

Introduction

When I was handed the task of writing this book, several memorable individual contributions to United's glory matches immediately sprang to mind. Gary Hamson's match-winning role in the League Cup win over mighty Liverpool in 1978 was one. Another obvious choice was Alan Kelly for his penalty shoot-out heroics in the FA Cup quarter-final victory against Coventry in 1998. And it was impossible to overlook Tony Currie's performance against West Ham in 1975, when his 'quality goal from a quality player' was thankfully captured by the *Match of the Day* cameras.

Currie is one of several former players featured who enjoy legendary status at the Lane. TC's old team-mates, classy full-back Len Badger and long-serving goalkeeper Alan Hodgkinson, would feature in any list of all-time United greats, along with prolific striker Keith Edwards. I should mention that, although Len is busy running his own pub, he kindly came over to my local, 'The Barrack' at Apperknowle, where we chatted over a couple of pints. (That plug must be worth a few pints, John!)

With the great United legend Jimmy Hagan now parading his skills on that great football pitch in the sky, two of his former team-mates, Colin Grainger and Tommy Hoyland, share their memories of playing alongside him. Similar glowing tributes are also paid to another Blades legend, Joe Shaw, who was sadly unavailable due to ill-health.

Cult hero Bob Booker would be the first to acknowledge that he wasn't blessed with the ability to compare with the likes of Hagan and Shaw, but he is fondly remembered by fans for his admirable battling qualities. I was sorry to learn of his departure from Brighton & Hove Albion just a few weeks after he took time out to meet me on the eve of Albion's game at Nottingham Forest.

No book featuring memorable Blades matches would be complete without an account of a victory over Wednesday. I considered contacting Bobby Davison to talk to him about his remarkable two-goal debut at Hillsborough, but instead decided to interview the scorer of the first goal that night, Dane Whitehouse. Dane's sheer joy at scoring in that game was still apparent as he described the goal in clear detail.

Born and bred in the Norton area of Sheffield, I started supporting the Blades as a boy. My first full season was the 1981/82 campaign, when United were in the bottom division for the first time in the proud history of the club. The League Cup victory over Arsenal that season was a particularly memorable match for me personally. I recall being thrown forward from my usual position in the centre of the Kop as fans celebrated Bob Hatton's winning goal. Keith Edwards and Tony Kenworthy were among my favourite players at that time, so I am pleased to be able to include their recollections and was delighted when Tony chose that game to reminisce over.

I would rate the unforgettable promotion-winning game at Leicester as the highlight from my time supporting the club. The sight of fans in a variety of fancy dress costumes invading the pitch every time United scored will be forever etched in my memory. Bob Booker had me in fits when he told his version of events, turning round after each of the five goals that day to be greeted by Mickey Mouse or a pantomime horse!

Each individual featured readily agreed to be interviewed, without personal reward, but the project was not without its setbacks. Several attempts to set up an interview with one former player fell through due to his busy work schedule and we eventually agreed it wasn't going to happen. Maybe next time. I was also disappointed at my failure to persuade another popular figure to co-operate. After making repeated requests, I was forced to admit defeat when the person in question decided, for reasons only known to himself, that he did not want to take part. Oh well, you can't win 'em all...

I would like to take this opportunity to mention a few people who have helped shape my interest in the Blades over the last quarter of a century. Mark Best and family took me to games in the early days and Roger Sharpe – a valued family friend for many years – also helped fuel my passion for the club. I have spent many, many hours discussing matters relating to the Blades in 'The Travellers Rest' at Apperknowle. (There's a bit of a theme emerging here. Well, what else is there in life, apart from football and alcohol?!)

I've regularly argued, sorry, chatted with Terry Maguire who has for many years taken a bus load of regulars to the Supporters Club's end of season presentation night at the Lane, whether they wanted to go or not! Other fellow Blades include Mike Brayshaw, Russ Dennett, Jamie Hamilton, Noel Hardwick, Gordon Harrison, Bob Janicki, Dave Leverton, Richard Long, Tony Long, Chris Marshall, Josie Marshall, Ken Perkins and Wayne Vaughan.

If this book gives you as much pleasure as I have had from writing it, I can only say it will have been a thundering good read.

Up the Blades!

Nick Johnson
September 2006

Foreword

DEREK DOOLEY

I know Nick Johnson personally, having been interviewed by him on a number of occasions, so I had no hesitation when he asked me to write the foreword for this book. *Match of My Life* brings together accounts of 12 memorable Blades matches over the last half-century, as told by players who featured prominently in those games. From Fifties and Sixties stars Colin Grainger, Alan Hodgkinson and Len Badger, via the likes of Tony Currie, Keith Edwards and Alan Kelly, to current favourite Phil Jagielka, this collection of stories will provide readers with a unique account of events that have gone down in Blades folklore.

One of the most memorable days for me personally was the promotion-winning game at Leicester. You couldn't have written the script for that match. Unbeknown to Dave Bassett, I'd arranged for the players' wives to come back to the Directors' Suite at Bramall Lane for a drink after the game. I told everyone not to let Dave know what I'd organised because he'd have crucified me. I was in the Leicester directors box and when they scored first, I felt so deflated. But I needn't have bothered because the players rolled their sleeves up and made it a great day. When we came back up the M1, cars were passing us, with fans tooting their horns. We went back to Bramall Lane and when Dave got off the coach, he had a few tears in his eyes, as we all did. They're the sort of days that you savour.

Bob Booker, who gives his account of the Leicester match in this book, thought he was going to leave at the end of that season. But we gave him a new deal and, not long afterwards, there was a knock on my door and in walked Bob who said, "I just wanted to thank you for giving me another contract." That made a welcome change because usually when players knocked on my door, it was to complain that they weren't being paid enough!

Before the away game against Wednesday in 1992, Bobby Davison joined us on loan. I'd arranged the loan agreement myself for Bobby to join us from Leeds United and we were paying him more than we were paying the others because you basically had to take the player's contract over. I spoke to fellow director Alan Laver before the game and he asked me whether we could afford the deal. "No, not really," I replied. Alan expressed doubts about the signing, but after Davison scored two goals, he came up to me and said he'd changed his opinion!

I can clearly recall the tension and drama of another game featured, the FA Cup quarter-final replay against Coventry, which went to a penalty shoot-out. They were brilliant penalties and of course Alan Kelly made some great saves. More recently, it was a tremendous finish to the game against Hull towards the end of the 2005/06 season that stirred the blood, picking up three points to virtually seal promotion.

Coming from the other side of the city, I was a little bit apprehensive when I first started working at Bramall Lane in 1974, wondering how Unitedites would react to me. I expected them to be saying, "Bloody Wednesdayite" and things like that, but they were really good and made me feel welcome. I think it's a bit unique that I'm respected by both sets of supporters in Sheffield and I have to pinch myself sometimes.

I am proud to have been involved with United for over thirty years. After joining the club as Commercial Manager, I worked my way up to the boardroom, taking on the role of Managing Director and then Chairman. When promotion was secured from the Championship, I thought it was a fitting time to announce my retirement. We were one of the founder members of the Premier League in 1992 and it was nice to get back there. Hopefully we can stay there, but I've been in football long enough to just accept what happens. I consider myself fortunate to have worked with Dave Bassett for eight years and Neil Warnock for six-and-a-half years. My relationship with both of them certainly helped to make my job easier.

You tend to forget about certain events until you read about them and it's nice to jog the memory. I am pleased to introduce this book which will provide fans with a reminder of some marvellous moments in the history of Sheffield United.

Derek Dooley MBE
September 2006

Dedication

This book is dedicated to Maria and my family: Mum and Dad, brother Mark, sister-in-law Helen, nephew William and niece Lucy. Thank you all for your love and support.

COLIN GRAINGER
LEFT WINGER 1953–1957

BORN   10 June 1933, Wakefield
SIGNED   July 1953 from Wrexham; £2,500
BLADES CAREER   95 games, 27 goals
HONOURS   7 England caps, 3 goals
LEFT   Transferred to Sunderland, February 1957; £23,000

A pacy winger who returned to his native South Yorkshire to sign for United after starting out at Wrexham. Colin's impressive form resulted in an England call-up and he scored twice on his debut against the mighty Brazil at Wembley. He was sold to Sunderland to help ease debts, with Sammy Kemp arriving at the club in part-exchange. Colin was known as the Singing Footballer after carving out a second career as a professional singer.

Barnsley 1 v Sheffield United 6

League Division Two
Saturday 1 September 1956

Oakwell
Attendance 21,189

Grainger hits hat-trick against his home-town club as the Blades record a
fifth straight win to maintain their 100 per cent start to the season

Teams

Tim Ward	**Managers**	Joe Mercer
Harry Hough	1	Ted Burgin
Barrie Betts	2	Cec Coldwell
Joe Thomas	3	Cliff Mason
Norman Smith	4	Tommy Hoyland
George Spruce	5	Joe Shaw
Henry Walters	6	Jim Iley
Arthur Kaye	7	Ronnie Waldock
Robert Wood	8	Jimmy Hagan
Lol Chappell	9	Derek Hawksworth
Malcolm Graham	10	Bobby Howitt
Frank Bartlett	11	Colin Grainger

Kaye 73	**Scorers**	Grainger 11, 26, 65
		Howitt 20, 84, Hawksworth 72

Referee: G Black

YOU COULD SAY football was in my blood. My brother Jack played for Rotherham and was an England 'B' international. My cousin Dennis Grainger was also an England 'B' international who played for Leeds, Wrexham and Oldham. And another cousin, Eddie Holliday, played for Sheffield Wednesday

I started out at Wrexham after cousin Dennis got me a trial there. I was 15 at the time and my dad took me down to play in a trial match. I understood it was a trial for the under-18s, but the right-back I was up against had a beard and I thought, "This lad's older than 17 or 18!" When there was a lull in the game, I asked him how old he was. "I'm 24," he replied. I thought it was a bit unfair, but I obviously did enough in the game because I was signed on by then manager Tom Williams.

I made my debut at the age of 17 against Hartlepool. I made only five league appearances for Wrexham because I was in the RAF and couldn't get many weekends off. I spent two years at the Racecourse Ground before Sheffield United signed me in the summer of 1953. While I was back at home, I received a telegram from Wrexham manager Peter Jackson, asking me to ring him because there was interest from United. He said, "We've had a formal offer from Sheffield United for your services, what do you think?" I told him I was interested because Sheffield was only twenty miles from home. I then met United manager Reg Freeman in a London hotel and signed up.

It was very exciting as United had just been promoted into the First Division as Second Division Champions. After making only a handful of appearances in my first season at Bramall Lane, I got more established the following term. I then missed only a few games during the 1955/56 season when we were relegated to Division Two after finishing at the bottom of the table. We were battling hard, but suffered four successive defeats and went down after losing against Tottenham. We'd finished 13th the previous season and it was a big disappointment to be relegated.

You might think it is strange, but I got called up to play for England against Brazil that summer. A local newspaper journalist called Ross

Jenkinson contacted me when I was in a London hotel and informed me of my call-up. "Congratulations, Colin," he said.

"What for?" I said.

"You've been picked to play against Brazil."

"Never."

"Yes, it's true. You've been named in the team."

Stanley Matthews had won a recall to the side at the age of 41 on the right wing and I changed alongside him in the dressing-room. Stanley was something of a loner and he used to eat his food in his hotel room instead of sitting with us. He stuck to a special diet and that helped him stay so fit so late in life. He had that aura, so you looked up to him. I thought he was brilliant.

I was trembling at the prospect of playing in front of a capacity 100,000 crowd at Wembley, but it turned out to be a dream debut. I scored with my first kick in the fifth minute. I was in a position near the back post, Johnny Haynes knocked the ball across and I ran onto it and fired into the net. Magic!

The big star for Brazil at that time was Didi who was the Pelé of that era and he scored the equaliser as they came back from 2-0 down to level. But Tommy Taylor put us back in front and I scored my second of the game late on, heading in a cross from Stanley Matthews to seal a 4-2 victory. Scoring two goals against Brazil on my England debut was something special. Representing England saw me playing with some of the finest players this country has ever produced. As well as Matthews, Duncan Edwards and Johnny Haynes also played against Brazil. We weren't able to see the best of Edwards, who would have been some player if he had not been killed in the Munich Air Disaster. He was powerful and strong and could shoot with such power, so 30-yard shots were nothing to him. You also have to remember that we were playing with a heavy leather ball back then. Haynes was another great player and he suited my game because he would knock accurate diagonal balls to me near the corner flag.

Playing against Wales at Wembley in November 1956, I broke my ankle and tore all the ligaments. I suffered with that for years and years, playing with the ankle strapped up. I still did all right, but I was always worried about going over on it. When the pitches were soft, it wasn't a problem. But when the pitches were dry and hard, I was always wary. My England career came to an end after I'd won seven caps.

Back on the domestic front, we set off like an express train at the start of the 1956/57 season. Jimmy Hagan and Jim Iley were on-form and I also enjoyed a good start to the season. I scored twice on the opening day at Rotherham and then twice in the following game at home to Fulham. I also scored from the penalty spot in the next game against Port Vale and had a chance to score a penalty at Fulham four days later, but I hit the cross-bar.

After winning our first four games, we were up against Barnsley and that had added appeal for me because they were my local team. I used to watch them during the war when they had guest players from other teams playing for them. I lived seven miles from Barnsley, so I'd get on the bus to the station in the centre of town and then run up to the ground. I'd make sure I got near the touchline so I could get a good view of stars like Danny Blanchflower and George Robledo who turned out for the Tykes.

I lived at Havercroft near Ryehill, which is seven miles from Barnsley. I remained there after getting married to Doreen because we lived with my mum and dad. I didn't have a car, so I had to travel to games in Sheffield by bus. For home matches I had to get the bus from Ryehill to Barnsley and then travel from there to Sheffield. After getting into the city, I'd then run and catch the tram to the Bramall Lane.

We had some bloody good players at United back then. Our goalkeeper, Ted Burgin, was very good. He was so agile, with tremendous reflexes. He lacked a little in height, but he made some marvellous saves and I rated him highly. He was also a great fella, who could make you laugh. His fingers were bent all over the place after they'd been broken and had not repaired properly through diving at forward's feet. But he'd take the knocks and get on with things. When we played at Everton in one game and won 2-1 in a famous victory, he had a superb match because they threw everything at him that day.

Cec Coldwell was a great servant to United. He was always very steady, rarely making a mistake. He wasn't the quickest, but he never broke sweat because he could read the game and had the positional sense to get into the right positions. Nobody ever took him to the cleaners. Cliff Mason was a happy-go-lucky type of defender. If he got the ball and saw someone up-field, he'd knock it long. He was quick, sharp and full of endeavour. Cliff was a good team man because if anybody beat him, he'd be up and at 'em again.

Tommy Hoyland was a footballing midfielder with good control. He wasn't the quickest, but he was comfortable on the ball and could pass it. He didn't carry the ball or get in advanced positions a lot, but he could play the ball when he had it and he'd compete as well. Like the others, he was also a nice, friendly lad. Joe Shaw couldn't get in the team for a while and he only emerged as a great player later his career. He was so sharp, with quick feet. I'd say Joe's reading of the game and anticipation was second to none. The ball was like a magnet to him; it would come to him somehow. He was the same in five-a-sides, just picking the ball up off you. Joe was neat and tidy on the ball and rarely gave it away. If he'd have been 6ft 2ins tall, I'd have said he'd have definitely played for England. But he was only about 5ft 8ins and I don't think England wanted to take a chance with him. Again, you couldn't wish to meet a nicer fella.

Jim Iley was powerful and strong with big legs. He was fit and mobile with good ability on the ball. The only time he gave it away was when he sometimes tried to play long, diagonal balls, which weren't on at times, so they'd get cut out. He went to Tottenham and then Newcastle and always did well. Jim played behind me and supplied me with some good balls. We trained together, going back in to do extra work in the afternoons because we really wanted to be professional footballers. He was a good friend and he finished up being my brother-in-law after marrying my sister.

Ronnie Waldock was a direct, powerful runner with a barrel chest. He used to play that way, driving forward. He would run through a brick wall and had a good shot. When balls were knocked over the top, Ronnie would be on to them. Again, he was a helluva nice kid. Derek Hawksworth had quick feet and he could shoot with either foot. He was quick and mobile and his goalscoring record was good.

Bobby Howitt was a typical Scottish player; neat and tidy with a helluva left foot. His shooting ability was brilliant because he could keep the ball low. He was always over the ball when he struck it. Bobby moved on to play with the legendary Stanley Matthews at Stoke City in the twilight of Matthews' incredible career.

The great Jimmy Hagan, who was about 32 when I first knew him, was injury prone because he was coming towards the end of his career. He had a superb touch and control, with very strong legs which enabled him to shield the ball. He didn't run very quickly, but with the ball at his feet he was brilliant. He could pick passes out even when he was coming to the end of his career. Jimmy was something special and I'd say he was the greatest-ever United player. He was always a part-timer because he used to teach, so he couldn't train full-time. He kept himself to himself and was a nice man, who never caused any trouble and never swore. You were always in awe of him because he'd done it all. We looked up to him because we knew if Jimmy was in-form, he'd get us through the game. He used to say, "It's up to you, Colin. You can take this full-back to the cleaners. Let's have a good game from you."

The last time I met Jimmy was at a Sheffield United match when he came over from Portugal around the early-Nineties. He caught my eye as I was about to take my seat and said, "Where are the wingers these days Colin?" I was proud to hear him say that because it proved to me that I must have been a decent player.

My England debut was an amazing experience – at Wembley and beating Brazil, but my favourite ever game for the Blades was this corker of a victory at Barnsley, made all the more special by it being in my home town.

That meant it was a comparatively short bus journey from Ryehill to the town centre for me, and, of course, I was travelling along with the Barnsley supporters, some of whom knew me.

Knowing that my family and a lot of people I'd grown up with would be there, I was desperate to put in a good performance. I didn't want people who knew me to go home and say, "Bloody hell, Colin Grainger was shocking." There were over 21,000 fans packed into Oakwell, which was a helluva gate then at Barnsley. They didn't even get that when they were in the Premiership. It was a typical local derby with the Barnsley players putting in some strong tackles early on. But we took the lead in the 11th minute when I scored following a Harry Hawksworth cross. I always liked to try and read the situation because I had a bit of ball sense, anticipating where the ball was going to go. When the ball came across from Hawksworth, I attacked it and struck a left-foot volley into the bottom corner of the net.

We then got well on top and I scored my second goal on 26 minutes, scoring from a similar position to the one I was in for the first goal, but this time I scored with a rare header. Jimmy Hagan took a corner and I met it with my head and directed it into the top corner. We were 3-0 up at half-time with Bobby Howitt also getting his name on the score-sheet.

I completed my hat-trick in the 65th minute following a run from the half-way line. Barnsley right-back Barrie Betts wasn't the quickest, but I was like lightning then, so I knocked the ball past him and ran with it, waiting for goalkeeper Harry Hough to come out. Hough sold himself and I rolled the ball past him into the far corner of the net. You get a kick out of scoring an individual goal like that. The hat-trick took my tally to eight goals in five games.

After Hawksworth made it 5-0 on 72 minutes, Arthur Kaye pulled a goal back for Barnsley a minute later. Howitt rounded off the scoring six minutes from time with his second of the game. To win 6-1 away from home was a good result. It was Barnsley's biggest defeat at Oakwell since pre-war days. We were simply too good for them that day. Jim Iley had a very good game and he was praised by manager Joe Mercer. For my part, I tore Barrie Betts to pieces. They had switched him from left-back specifically to face me, but it didn't work because he had a shocker. Being from the area, I knew Barrie and he was a nice lad. He was also a nice footballer and not the type who could clog you. He later went on to Manchester City.

Scoring a hat-trick makes you feel as though you've really achieved something and I was proud I'd done it. When the game is over and you know you've performed, it's a wonderful feeling. I was full of it and on cloud nine, but there was no fancy sports car waiting for me to drive home in. People don't appreciate now what it was like when I was playing. After having a shower, I walked to the bus station on my own, picked up a copy of the *Green 'Un* newspaper and read about the game after getting on the bus. I was sat there with the Barnsley supporters, talking about the match. There were one or two comments like, "You were lucky" or whatever. I didn't get any stick, as such, from the Barnsley fans, but they didn't like what had happened. My childhood friends were there, supporting Barnsley. After I'd scored the hat-trick, they said, "Well you've done a dirty trick. I'm surprised at you, taking us to the cleaners." But there was no ill-feeling. In any case, what could I do? I had a job to do and you have to take the goals if they come. I don't think it was a coincidence that I had a great game every time I played at Barnsley. I drove myself on and chased everything when I played there.

In the local paper, above the match report for the Barnsley game, the headline read: 'COUNT THEM AS BACK', referring to the belief that United were favourites to return to the First Division after such a fantastic start to the season. But talk of making an immediate return to the top-flight proved to be premature as our form dipped alarmingly, winning only once in our next six matches. I was sold the following February and United finished in seventh place, which was very disappointing after such an impressive start to the season.

I used to get a lot of stick from defenders. They used to tell me in advance what they were going to do, saying, "I've been told to kick you." I'd say, "Thank you very much!" If you go near a player now, it's a free-kick, but in my day you could tackle from behind with a bit of follow-through. Players in the current game will try and waste time by taking the ball to the corner flag and keeping it there, but you daren't do that in my day because you'd have been up in the air. One of the hardest players around at that time was Eddie Stuart of Wolves who was a big South African. He was strong and powerful and he used to hit you.

The balls are so light now and the boots are so light. If you get kicked, the boots can't hurt you because they're soft and there's nothing there. The boots were heavy when I was playing and even the studs were made of leather, so if they caught your shin, you were cut. It's a different game altogether now. Players are very limited in their ability at going past people. Wayne Rooney and Joe Cole can go past people, but there aren't any others in the England team who can do that, particularly David Beckham. It's a lost art now because they're told to pass the ball and retain possession. We had to run with the ball at our feet and take people on because if you didn't, you'd get a rollocking at half-time.

There were no real systems in those days, we just used to go out and play. You knew the position you were playing in and got on with it. I didn't need anybody on the touchline to tell me what I had to do. If the ball was in the attacking third, I had to get level with it. If the ball was knocked back, I'd go back to get level with it. That's how I used to operate because if you're level with the ball, you're in play. If you're defending, you get the ball from the keeper. But if you're stood on the half-way line, you can't get the ball from the keeper, can you?

I thought that United manager Joe Mercer was a brilliant fella. He was like a fatherly figure because he took to me. He was my mentor, giving me one-on-one coaching on the training pitch in the afternoons. He'd show me what I had to do in different positions on the pitch, telling me when to cross the ball and things like that. He used to push me and gave me a lot of confidence. He'd say to other managers, "This lad's going to play for England." When he went to Aston Villa, he wanted me to go with him to Villa Park. "You'd just suit us, playing on a big pitch," he said. But nothing happened because United wouldn't let me go at that particular time.

The only reason I eventually left the Blades was because they were short of money. They had to find £5,000 within seven days because the bank was putting pressure on and I was the only asset they had. I didn't want to go, but I was told by the directors that I had to because they needed the money.

I moved to Sunderland in February 1957 in a deal worth a total of £23,000, which was a lot of money at that time, in fact just £2,000 shy of the then transfer record for Jackie Sewell. United received £17,000 plus a player called Sammy Kemp. Sunderland was the 'Millionaire Club' then with stars like Len Shackleton, Billy Bingham, Don Revie, Ray Daniel and Charlie Fleming. Shackleton was the really big star up there. He could spin the ball and make it come back to him. But somehow, despite having some great players, we got relegated that season. The problem was that we just used to play as individuals instead of playing as a team. Whoever got the ball would do their bit with it.

After three years at Sunderland, I moved on to Leeds United for £15,000, which was a record fee for them at that time. The likes of Jack Charlton, Billy Bremner and Don Revie were there, but I didn't enjoy it one bit at Elland Road. Manager Jack Taylor was a lovely fella, but he was quiet and wasn't a leader, so nobody took any notice of him. When Revie became manager, I left because I knew too much about him after playing with him at Sunderland. I wanted to go anyway because I wasn't enjoying it, so I went to Port Vale. After there, I finished my career with two seasons at Doncaster Rovers. I was 33 when I packed in playing. I felt I'd just come to the end of the road because I wasn't playing with players who could give you the ball.

I was already well established in my second career as a singer by the time I hung up my boots. I used to sing in the dressing-room and, when I was on tour with the England squad in Finland, there was a dinner featuring a cabaret act in Helsinki and Nat Lofthouse got me up to sing. It went from there and I sang all over the country after that. I sang at a packed Sheffield Empire and also performed in places like Liverpool, Leeds, Newcastle and Glasgow. Empire theatres were big and popular at the time and could easily hold a thousand people.

I was once on the same bill as The Beatles at the Southern Sporting Club in Manchester. I also stood in for Ronnie Hilton at the Newcastle Empire and Des O'Connor was on the same bill. At a time when I was earning £20-a-week from football, I'd get £100 for doing a show, which was a lot of money. My second career went very well. We once sold out the Sunderland Empire for a run of shows I did with my colleague at Roker Park, Stan Anderson. I'd get a little more nervous preparing for a show than before playing in a football match. When you're on a stage, any mistakes you make are down to you whereas someone can cover for you on a football pitch.

I'd get on the train at eight o'clock on Monday morning and go down to London for a half-hour voice coaching session with an Italian who was also the tutor to Harry Secombe. Al Jolson was my favourite artiste, but I would say my style was somewhere between Tom Jones and Engelbert Humperdink.

As well as doing cabaret, I recorded for HMV and only just missed out on breaking into the charts.

I appeared on TV in the Winifred Attwell Show and the Hughie Green Show. I was very unlucky because I'd just got going when the likes of Bill Haley, Tommy Steele and Lonnie Donnegan came on the scene, so it went from the kind of ballads that I was singing to rock 'n' roll, which killed us ballad singers. I got a bit sick of all the travelling because my wife and I had a young family to bring up, so I packed up as a full-time singer and just did it part-time, singing in Sheffield clubs and other places locally. I got a job as a salesman, selling wines and spirits. It was a steady living and I did that for about twenty years before retiring in 1994.

I've been involved in football in a scouting capacity since 1979. I started scouting for Billy Bingham at Mansfield. After a spell at Barnsley, I scouted for Allan Clarke at Leeds. Then I went to Huddersfield when Mick Buxton was manager and spent 14 years there. I linked up with Neil Warnock when he went to Huddersfield and I've worked with him for 11 years. I was at Bury and Plymouth with him before he took over at Bramall Lane, so I'm now back at United. I do a lot of reports for Neil, checking out players he's interested in. He'll give me a phone call and ask me to look at a particular player he's thinking of signing. I enjoy the job and it's great to still be involved at Bramall Lane after all these years because my time at United was definitely the high point in my career.

TOMMY HOYLAND
WING-HALF 1949–1961

BORN   14 June 1932, Sheffield
SIGNED   October 1949 from Apprentice
BLADES CAREER   198 games, 14 goals
HONOURS   Division Two Championship 1952/53 & 1960/61
LEFT   Transferred to Bradford City, October 1961

Starting out as an inside-forward, Tommy struggled to hold down a regular place in the side. He flourished after being switched to wing-half, with his pace and strong tackling put to good effect in the new role. Tommy was proud to see his son Jamie follow in his footsteps and play for the Blades, putting them among only a handful of father and sons to have done so.

West Ham United 0 v Sheffield United 3

League Division Two
Monday 9 September 1957

Upton Park
Attendance 21,746

Hoyland hat-trick ensures impressive victory for Blades over eventual champions West Ham on their own turf

Teams

Ted Fenton	**Managers**	Joe Mercer
Brian Rhodes	1	Alan Hodgkinson
John Bond	2	Cec Coldwell
Noel Cantwell	3	Graham Shaw
Malcolm Pyke	4	Brian Richardson
Ken Brown	5	Joe Shaw
Andrew Malcolm	6	Gerry Summers
Michael Grice	7	Sammy Kemp
Eddie Lewis	8	Tommy Hoyland
William Dare	9	Bobby Howitt
Alan Blackburn	10	Billy Russell
Malcolm Musgrove	11	Derek Hawksworth
	Scorers	Hoyland 18, 65, 90

Referee: C Kingston

I HAVE CHOSEN THE game at West Ham in September 1957 as the most memorable match I featured in for United, due to the fact that I scored a hat-trick that day. But ironically, that period really marked the beginning of the end for me as a United player, even though I spent four more years at the club.

After finishing seventh in the Second Division at the end of the previous campaign, despite having a great start, we experienced a mixed start to the 1957/58 season. We won at home to Notts County on the opening day, lost at Charlton and drew at Lincoln. We then suffered a 3-0 defeat at home to Charlton before beating Bristol Rovers. West Ham had made a better start, losing only once in their opening five games – which was away at Blackburn – before facing us.

I began that season as a wing-half, a position I had occupied since being switched from inside-forward during the 1954/55 season. I found it easy to make the change and it was really only then that I held down a firm place in the side. I was a virtual ever-present during that season, so my career took off in the new role. Trainer Ernest Jackson had been a wing-half and he'd obviously talked to manager Reg Freeman about the possibility of me changing to a different position.

Joe Mercer, who replaced Freeman as manager in August 1955, also mainly used me as a wing-half. But the great Jimmy Hagan stood down for the Bristol Rovers match on the Saturday because he was struggling with the pace of the game at the age of 39, so I reverted to inside-forward, with Brian Richardson taking over at wing-half. I retained my place in attack for the trip to West Ham as Mercer made just one change with Sammy Kemp replacing Alf Ringstead.

We got off to a really good start at Upton Park and I scored after 18 minutes to put us in front. I raced on to a pass from inside-left Bobby Howitt around the half-way line and advanced towards goal before beating goalkeeper Brian Rhodes with a rising drive from a narrow angle.

We held on to our lead going into the break and knew that West Ham would be coming at us in the second-half. Sure enough, backed by their noisy supporters, they threw men forward in numbers and really went for it in a bid to get back on level terms. West Ham had a couple of pacy wingers in Michael Grice and Malcolm Musgrove, who provided some good crosses, but Joe Shaw was there to chest them down, providing goalkeeper Alan Hodgkinson with solid protection. Joe was a beautiful player who was very unfortunate to not win an England cap. Graham Shaw, who was a big pal of mine, also had a good game.

When the West Ham forwards did manage to get through the defence, Hodgkinson pulled off several great saves. Alan was a very good goalkeeper, who of course played for England. In fact he had made his international debut in a 2-1 win against Scotland. As the home side came under increasing pressure to pull a goal back, 'Hodgy' was on the receiving end of a rough challenge from inside-forward Eddie Lewis. As Alan came out to claim the ball, he was double-charged by Lewis and had to receive treatment before carrying on. To give you an idea of how bad the challenge was, Lewis found himself in the unusual position of being booed by his own supporters!

We managed to keep West Ham at bay with Bobby Howitt playing some good balls to me and Billy Russell. Sammy Kemp and Derek Hawksworth also worked hard, causing problems for the opposition with their prompting. With West Ham throwing players forward it gave us space to hit back on the break. Hawksworth had a hand in the second goal, which was a little scrappy. After the ball was played in from the wing, Derek's shot was blocked and I got on the end of the rebound.

At 2-0 we had a bit of a cushion and there was further pressure on West Ham to try and get back into the game. But they failed to find a way through and I sealed my hat-trick in the last minute. After short passes were played between Howitt and Kemp, the ball ran loose in the goal-mouth and I was on hand to turn the ball home.

The headline at the top of the match report in the Sheffield Telegraph the following morning read, 'Sheffield United Set Off Own Brand Of 'H' Bomb.' Dave Pardon wrote, 'Sheffield United exploded their own brand of 'H' bomb in London last night – the 'H' for Hoyland Hat-trick. It sent morale sky-high and raised the roof of Upton Park after 90 minutes of heart-warming football.'

It was a great feeling to score a hat-trick, especially against such a strong side. West Ham didn't lose another game at home that season as they went on to win the Second Division title. The usual custom for scoring a hat-trick was to be presented with the match-ball, signed by all the players from the game, but I didn't receive it, which was disappointing. Neither did I receive any congratulations, or even an acknowledgement of what I had done, from my own manager, Joe Mercer. I knew then that I wasn't really the flavour of the month as far as he was concerned.

I didn't like Mercer, to be honest. He had been a great player for Everton and Arsenal and also captained England. But as a person, I found him to be two-faced. After one game, he came up to me in the dressing room, put his arm round me and said, "I'll get you a cap this year." He then dropped me a few games later! That's how he was. I also remember after losing 5-0 at Leicester in 1957, we went into the dressing-room at full-time and he laughed at us. A Leicester player called John Morris, who'd previously been at Manchester United, knew Mercer and popped his head round the dressing room door to say goodbye to him. Mercer turned towards him and said, "What a load of so-and-sos, I've got here." I didn't think it was right to say something like that to an opposing player in front of us.

Joe Shaw played as an inside-right that day and Mercer wanted to get rid of Joe at that time. He also tried to sell Graham Shaw to Stoke, but he wouldn't go because he was happy at United. Mercer didn't want players like Joe and Graham who could play, which was funny because he'd been a stylish footballer himself. He wanted players at the back to just get the ball out of the area. Malcolm Barrass was brought in from Bolton and he fitted that mould. Malcolm was a smashing chap, but he struggled and was dropped with Joe Shaw winning a recall in his place.

When Mercer dropped me, he asked me whether I wanted to be the 12th man on the Saturday or play in the reserves. "I want to play in the reserves and try to get back in," I told him. That plan didn't do anything to improve my chances because the reserves played at Liverpool and got a right stuffing! The only credit I can give Mercer was for putting a solid defence together. Brian Richardson came in as my replacement and there was Joe Shaw, Graham Shaw and Cec Coldwell, so it was a very solid unit.

For me, Jimmy Hagan has got to be United's greatest-ever player. The game at Derby, which was just five days after the West Ham match, proved to be Jimmy's final appearance before retiring. A lot of people thought Jimmy was a bit aloof, but he was a big help to me. He was a fabulous player, who was unfortunate to be around when there were terrific players like Raich Carter and Wilf Mannion on the scene, otherwise he'd have had a bundle of England caps. As it was, he only won one cap.

Jimmy would often tell me things in confidence. I remember talking to him after he turned down a chance to join Sheffield Wednesday for a

£32,500 fee at the age of 33. That would have been a transfer record at the time – for a 33 year-old! The conversation took place when we were on the train going up to Clyde to play in a Sheffield versus Glasgow game. "There was no point in me going to Wednesday," he said. "I couldn't have achieved anything for myself by going there because if they went down, they'd crucify me." There was huge rivalry between the two clubs and fans, of course, just as there is today and Jimmy didn't want to fall foul of that and become the target for blame if Wednesday didn't do so well.

With the maximum wage in force, there was no financial gain to be had from going to another club back then either, unless you received a back-hander, of course – and that sort of thing did go on. I know a few clubs did do a bit of fiddling including Sunderland, who were punished.

My football education began at Southey Green School and I played for Sheffield Boys as a right-back, captaining the team when I was 13 or 14. Southey Green School had the best school team in the city at the time. Graham Shaw went to the same school, although he was two years younger than me. We lived on the same road when we were kids and remained close friends up until his death eight years ago. He actually played in goal as a kid before being moved to full-back.

I went to Oaks Fold, which was classed as United's nursery team, after leaving school at 14. After about 12 months with Oaks Fold, I started training with United on Tuesday and Thursday nights. I continued to turn out for Oaks Fold until I started playing for the United 'A' team at the age of 16. Reg Wright and Arthur Eggleston trained the youngsters and Teddy Davison was the manager. I played only briefly under Teddy who was a very quiet man.

I received a first-team call-up at the age of 17, playing against Leicester and getting my name on the score-sheet. Fred Smith nodded down to Harold Brook who played me in and I fired in a shot from the edge of the box, with the ball flying into the top corner of the net in front of the Kop. I'll never forget that goal.

The rest of the players looked after me. Harold Brook, who was ten years older than me, was a really big help. That season we failed to win promotion by 0.008 of a goal, with Sheffield Wednesday going up instead of us. That was gutting. Wednesday played Tottenham on the last day of the season and they say it was the biggest cut-up ever, with Tottenham players missing the target from a yard out! If Wednesday had drawn 1-1, we'd have gone up, but they drew 0-0.

I did my National Service, spending two years in the Army at Oswestry at the start of the 1950s. After coming out of the Army, I was frustrated because I was having a lean spell and couldn't get back in the side. I remember on one occasion blowing my top with trainer Ernest Jackson in training. Harold Brook, who saw what had happened, came up to me to offer his advice. "Look, if he's shouting at you it's because you're doing something wrong, so just listen," he said. That was typical of 'Brooky' and I'll never forget those words.

After United won promotion to the First Division in 1952/53, I came in and played a few games as an inside-forward. Reg Freeman had taken over as manager from Teddy Davison. Reg, who came to the club from Rotherham United, was a lovely chap. Like Teddy, he wasn't the type to shout and bawl. At that time, there was a long row of hot copper pipes as you went into the dressing-room at Bramall Lane and Reg used to go up to the pipes and rub his back against them to get warm. After finishing mid-table in the 1954/55 season, we were shocked by the death of Reg over the summer. He was ill with cancer and went very quickly.

Joe Mercer was appointed as the new manager just before the start of the following season. Four successive defeats sent us down to Division Two at the end of the following campaign. That was sickening because we'd done well at Easter, beating Everton and drawing in the return match. We also beat Chelsea and drew at Blackpool, so we thought we'd survive. But defeats against Manchester City, Aston Villa, Sunderland and Tottenham saw us relegated. I was dropped from the side for the last game of the season away at white Hart Lane.

I only missed a few games in 1956/57 as we finished seventh in Division Two, but the following season was the beginning of the end for me as far as my United career was concerned because Brian Richardson took my place in the side. After the West Ham game, despite scoring that hat-trick, I made only a handful of appearances that term.

Following an injury to Brian, I did have a good run in the team during the 1958/59 season and we should have got to the FA Cup Final that year. I can remember when we faced Arsenal at Bramall Lane in the fifth round replay. It was a midweek game and I had to be down at the ground for 6.30pm, with the kick-off an hour later. I got on the tram at Sheffield Lane Top and there was a blanket of fog as we reached Wicker Arches, delaying our journey. I was getting increasingly worried about being late, so I jumped off the tram and ran to Bramall Lane, getting there at about 7pm! It's funny when you think nowadays about players driving to matches in their expensive sports cars.

After beating Arsenal 3-0 that night, we faced Norwich at home in the sixth round. Norwich were in the Third Division at that time, so we were firm favourites to go through to the semi-finals. We took an early lead and the Norwich goalkeeper, Ken Nethercott, suffered a dislocated shoulder with half an hour left. But he carried on and they scored an equaliser to force a replay. We played well down there, but lost 3-2. It was particularly galling to go out as the final that year was Nottingham Forest against Luton. We could have beaten either of those teams.

Joe Mercer resigned on Christmas Eve that season to take over at Aston Villa. I was with Graham Shaw when we heard the news that he had walked out. We were preparing for a game at Grimsby on Christmas Day morning and chief scout Archie Clark became the caretaker-manager. John Harris took over as manager towards the end of the season and we just missed out on promotion, finishing third. John, whose previous job was at Chester, was a very good manager. He was a very deep man, but I liked him because he was honest. He was religious and never swore, 'blummin' was as far as he went when he was unhappy about something. I played against John when he was at Chelsea and he was as hard as nails on the pitch.

After growing up with Graham Shaw, we became neighbours again in 1960. I lived in a club house at Sheffield Lane Top at that time, paying a pound a week rent. Graham lived in Beauchief and I asked him to keep an eye out for a house in the area. He told me that one of his neighbours, who was a bank manager, was selling his house to move up to Scotland with his job. Graham spoke to him and he said it would be okay to go over to see the house that night. I got the tram across to Meadowhead and cut through Chancet Wood. I'd bought the house by twenty to six; it was all done and dusted and I paid £2,200 for it! We were only in it for 12 months because we bought a newsagents at Greenhill. I sold the house for £2,400 and thought I'd won the pools because £200 was a lot of money in those days.

I made only a handful of appearances in my last two seasons at the club. We won promotion to Division One and I played just once early in the following season before moving to Bradford City in October 1961. I knew that I wasn't going to be playing regularly for United when Bradford came in for me. John Harris told me that Bradford were interested in signing me, so I spoke to their manager, Bob Brocklebank, and signed for them on the Friday before playing for them the following day. David 'Bronco' Layne, who later went to Sheffield Wednesday and was banned from playing for his part in the famous 'match-fixing' scandal, was in the Bradford side. I played a couple of seasons there before signing for Retford in the Midland League, where I had an enjoyable season. Someone gave me a whack on the knee which caused a ligament problem, keeping me out for about eight weeks and when the manager left at the end of the season, former Sheffield Wednesday player Dennis Woodhead took over. I knew Dennis very well and he told me that he couldn't keep me because I was on £25-a-week, which was a lot of money then for playing in the Midland League. I then had spells at Alfreton and Worksop before packing in altogether.

After running the newsagents for 15 years, my wife and I took over the Sheldon Pub in 1976. It was very busy on match-days and we had eight people serving behind the bar at one time. We never stood for swearing, which the customers respected, so we never had any trouble when we were there. We were at the Sheldon until retiring in 1992.

I've got three lads who were all football crazy and one of them, Jamie, played for United. There haven't been many father and sons who've played for the club. He started out at Manchester City and then played for Bury before joining United. I was always a little bit on edge when I watched him play because I know how fickle fans can be. They can be cruel at times, but I used to take it with a pinch of salt. He scored against Manchester United in the FA Cup at Bramall Lane in 1993 when the Blades won 2-1.

Jamie was very lucky because he could have lost his life due to a blood clot. He'd been to a private hospital in Manchester after getting injured in a game and on the way home he was in a lot of pain, so he went back to the hospital and was told he could have died. Jamie now coaches at Burnley's Academy and works for Mitre as a representative, travelling to various clubs.

Our Andrew is the deputy headmaster at Stocksbridge High School. He was on Sheffield Wednesday's books and was a good full-back. Graham was with Sheffield Wednesday and Chesterfield as a kid and was going to sign as a pro for Blackburn, but that fell through when Bobby Saxton was sacked as manager. He played for various non-league clubs including Matlock Town.

I'm involved with the Senior Blades Club at Bramall Lane and we have regular lunch-time meetings featuring different guest speakers. I go to most of United's home games. I started going regularly because our eldest grandson Thomas, who is Graham's son, is a Unitedite. I've always gone to games, but I often played golf on a Saturday until our Tom started wanting to go to matches and he got me going again. That was the season when we got to the Play-off final and lost against Wolves. People were telling me how well they were playing, so I went to the final and we lost. I went down to the match on a coach with our Tom. They were never in it that day. After the game, we got back to the coach and nobody talked about what had happened. So it's great to see United back in the top-flight and I'm looking forward to seeing the big names playing at Bramall Lane.

ALAN HODGKINSON
GOALKEEPER 1953–1971

BORN   16 August 1936, Maltby, Rotherham
SIGNED   August 1953 from Worksop Town
BLADES CAREER   652 games
HONOURS   Promoted from Division Two 1960/61 & 1970/71,
5 England caps, 7 England U23 caps
LEFT   Retired 1971

A true Blades legend, Alan made up for his lack of height with a superb technique and excellent agility. He was United's first-choice goalkeeper for 14 years and his association with the club spanned 22, following a spell on the coaching staff after retirement. 'Hodgy' went on to become the first specialist goalkeeping coach in the country, working with various clubs including Manchester United and Glasgow Rangers, along with the Scotland team. At the age of 70, he is still involved in the game at Oxford United.

Newcastle United 1 v Sheffield United 3

FA Cup Sixth Round
Saturday 4 March 1961

St. James's Park
Attendance 54,640

Second Division Blades win comfortably at First Division Newcastle to secure an FA Cup semi-final place for the first time since 1936.

Teams

Charlie Mitten	**Managers**	John Harris
Stewart Mitchell	1	Alan Hodgkinson
William McKinney	2	Cec Coldwell
Alf McMichael	3	Graham Shaw
Duncan Neale	4	Brian Richardson
William Thompson	5	Joe Shaw
Jackie Bell	6	Gerry Summers
Gordon Hughes	7	Bill Hodgson
Ivor Allchurch	8	Billy Russell
Len White	9	Doc Pace
John McGuigan	10	Keith Kettlebrough
Albert Scanlon	11	Ronnie Simpson
McGuigan 84	**Scorers**	Russell 6, 12, 18

Referee: K Collinge

THERE WAS THE harsh reality of my father working down the pit when I was growing up in Rotherham. We always had a piano in the back room and I was sent for piano lessons in the hope that I'd become a concert pianist, but I would take the shilling for my lesson and go and play football on the recreation ground with the rest of the lads instead. It got me into loads of trouble. When the lady who taught me piano saw my father, she'd say, "He never came last week." My parents weren't best pleased. I did eventually take a couple of piano exams, but I couldn't carry on playing because football took over.

Reg Freeman was the manager who signed me for United, bringing me to the club from Worksop Town. Reg was a really lovely, unassuming guy, who took his time to assess me. I played in a friendly against Clyde in April 1954, which was the first game under floodlights at Bramall Lane.Later that same month, I also played in a testimonial match at Northampton. I then travelled on an end of season tour of Germany, shortly after signing as a professional. United had just won promotion to the First Division and first-choice goalkeeper Ted Burgin was away with the England squad at the World Cup in Switzerland. Ted was a very agile keeper and I learned a lot of things from him. When we first met, I can remember shaking hands with him and noticing that his fingers were all bent. It was unbelievable and I thought, "How did he get fingers like that?" When I watched him play, he would always punch the ball instead of catching it and I think that's why his fingers were all shapes. I felt at that time that if I wanted to go a long way in the game, I had to work on good technique. As a coach I've worked with top keepers like Peter Schmeichel, Peter Shilton, Neville Southall and David Seaman and my work consists of great technique. If you can develop a great technique, your fingers stay straight, keeping your hands in good shape.

I made my league debut at Newcastle in August 1954, in front of a crowd of over 52,000. Newcastle had started the season very well, winning at Arsenal and then comfortably winning at home against West Brom before facing us in the third game. It was an awesome game to make my debut in, with players like Jackie Milburn and Ronnie Simpson in the Newcastle side. Simpson, the Scotland goalkeeper, was my hero and every time his picture appeared in the paper, I'd cut it out and stick it in a scrapbook. Like me, he was quite small for a goalkeeper.

We travelled up on the train on the Friday night and I was sat there in the carriage with senior players like Joe Shaw and Fred Furniss. As I was quiet and clearly apprehensive, Joe came up to me and asked, "Are you all right, Alan?"

"Aye, I'm all right," I replied.

"You're quiet."

"Well, it's going to be quite big for me."

"Look," he said, "if you don't make a debut, you never play, do you?"

It was great advice and his words relaxed me a little bit, putting me on the straight road for playing the following day. I think it was Joe Shaw's first game at centre-half, so we were up against the likes of Milburn, Bob Stokoe, Alf McMichael and Vic Keeble with a small centre-half and a small goalkeeper, which sounds ominous, but we ended up winning 2-1.

After playing in the following ten games, I then went off to do my National Service. I played in the Army team, which was full of internationals, including Bobby Charlton, Duncan Edwards, Jimmy Armfield, Peter Swan, Graham Shaw and Trevor Smith. I played in every Army game for two years and received some good write-ups. Joe Mercer, who by then had taken over from Reg Freeman as United manager, used to watch the Army matches and he sent for me while I was still doing my National Service after deciding to put me in the first-team. I never looked back after getting in during the second-half of the 1956/57 season, staying in the side right up until the Seventies.

Things changed quickly for me because I started playing regularly for United in January 1957, came out of the forces the following month and played for England in April. I think I'm still the smallest goalkeeper ever to have played for England. United remained in the Second Division over the following few seasons and, after Joe Mercer's resignation at Christmas in 1958, chief scout Archie Clark was in charge for a few games. Archie was a lively character and a super guy. He was a stocky man, who always wore a trilby hat. John Harris then took over as manager and he was different to anybody else I've ever met. He was a typical Scotsman, really. If you went in for a pay rise, he used to say that he'd love to give you more money, but the FA wouldn't allow it. Alternatively, he'd tell you to turn a light off at home or only have one bar lit on your gas fire! John was a quiet man who called a spade a spade.

He was very fortunate in respect that he took over a group of players which was ready-made for him. The team he selected was basically the same all the time; it was only the forwards who changed occasionally. Mercer set up a great defence with Cec Coldwell, Joe Shaw, Gerry Summers and Brian Richardson playing in front of me and we stayed together for about seven seasons. We played 42 league matches a year and it was very rare that any of us missed a game. Consistency was the key. It was like clock-work and we never got beaten heavily.

It was a great time for United because we used to have good runs in the FA Cup. We got to the quarter-finals practically every year and we used to beat First Division clubs even when we were in the Second Division. I particularly remember going to Spurs in the fourth round in the 1957/58 season and winning 3-0 when they had a good side, which would, three years later, develop into the team which won the first League and Cup double for sixty years.

The game I've chosen as the Match of My Life came during a particularly good Cup run in that 1960/61 season when Bill Nicholson's Tottenham side swept all before them. Following an impressive 1-0 win at First Division Everton in the third round, we progressed to the quarter-finals after knocking out Lincoln City and Blackburn Rovers and were drawn away to Newcastle. With Wednesday also in the quarter-finals, there was the prospect of an all-Sheffield final, but that really didn't come into our thinking at all. We weren't bothered about what other people were doing and to be successful, that's how you have to be. We were focused on the Newcastle match and just got on with it. I think one of the great words in sport is 'focus'. It's a small word, but it's one hell of a world-wide thing. You have to focus on what you're going to do in a game or during every second of whatever sport you're taking part in if you want to be successful.

It was a very daunting experience going up to Newcastle as the memories of their great Cup winning exploits during the 1950s, when they had lifted the trophy three times, were fresh in the mind and everyone was a bit apprehensive. We travelled up on the Friday night and stayed in Durham, where we went to the cinema and watched *Ben Hur*. Of course, we were thinking how nice it would be to get into the FA Cup semi-finals, but we were also in the running for promotion from the Second Division. It was between us and Ipswich for the title and they ended up winning it, with us as the runners-up.

We were all up for the game on the Saturday morning. We went out onto the pitch with the attitude that we had nothing to lose as we were certainly huge underdogs. Billy Russell gave us a great start when he scored after only six minutes. Gerry Summers lofted the ball forward to Bill Hodgson whose header into the goalmouth was dropped by goalkeeper Stewart Mitchell and Billy Russell was on-hand to turn the ball home.

Our dream start continued as it became 2-0 in the 12th minute, with Russell again the scorer. After seeing his shot cannon off defender Jackie Bell, Ronnie Simpson played the ball to Russell who fired past Mitchell. Incredibly Russell completed his hat-trick just six minutes later. Hodgson headed against a post, Simpson picked up the loose ball and went past William Thompson before setting up Russell for a fairly simple finish. To cap it all, Russell was a school teacher, who taught German at Wythenshawe Technical High School and played as a part-timer. I think that must have been the pinnacle of his career. It was certainly a wonderful moment and an unbelievable way for us to start the game.

We threatened to go further ahead before half-time with Mitchell twice called into action to keep out the very lively Russell. Then, with Mitchell out of position, McMichael was forced to clear the ball off the line from a Hodgson header.

At the other end, we were very well-organised at the back, so Newcastle never really threatened to make a comeback. It wasn't that we played defensively, but we had a great understanding and great self-belief. Joe Shaw was superb that day. I played with Joe for many years and he was a super, super guy. He was without doubt the best uncapped player around during my career. Joe was the first 'sweeper' in British football. He could anticipate what a centre-forward was going to do and I never saw big players like Derek Dougan beat him in the air. I remember when we played at Leeds, Don Revie pushed Jack Charlton up to centre-forward because of the fact that Joe was small and I was a small goalkeeper. But Joe had Big Jack in his pocket and in fact Jack says in his autobiography that it was one of the most embarrassing afternoons he had in football. I have great memories of Joe and I respected him immensely. We had a great understanding; it was like telepathy. I used to know what he was going to do and he knew what I was going to do.

Cec Coldwell and Graham Shaw also did well to plug any holes at the back. Cec, who took over the captaincy from Joe Shaw, was an outstanding captain. In fact, I would think he was one of the best skippers that United have ever had. Graham was another outstanding player. You have to have a level of consistency. It's no good having a good game one week, a poor one the next and then an ordinary one. All the top players in the world have a consistency level which makes them internationals. At club level, they have a consistent performance level and that's what we had with the defensive set-up in that era. It was very rare that we conceded more goals than we played matches and from my point of view, I thought I contributed a lot to that. All great teams have good units at the back. Arsenal had that in the Nineties and Chelsea have got it now. It makes such a difference, because you've got the understanding there.

Newcastle's defence just couldn't cope that day with Russell and Keith Kettleborough through the middle and Hodgson and Simpson down the wings. Doc Pace also caused problems for Thompson. Doc was a wonderful guy and a great competitor. In those days, they never used to put matches off because it was frosty or the pitch was rock hard. They'd put a bit of peat down in the six-yard box for the goalies, but you just got on with it and played. Doc was the kind of guy who'd dive in, whatever the conditions, to score goals. It was unbelievable the lengths he'd go to hit the back of the net. Doc was a great team-man and we all had great admiration for him.

Newcastle did manage to score six minutes from time, when John McGuigan beat me after getting on the end of a long ball from Albert Scanlon, but it was too late in the game to suggest it was going to be anything other than a consolation goal. We played exceptionally well, we really did. Winning at Newcastle was a great highlight in my career. After the game, it was a great journey as we headed back to Sheffield.

We faced top six First Division side Leicester City in the semi-finals and had quite a tussle with them. We played the first game at Elland Road, Leeds and they had ten men for most of the game after losing a winger called Gordon Wills through injury, but we just couldn't beat them. With virtually the last kick of the game, Doc Pace took a cross down on his chest and rammed the ball past Gordon Banks. I was at the other end thinking, "we're at Wembley!" but the referee, dear old Jim Finney, ruled-out the goal. He said Doc had handled the ball. We were all convinced that Doc had scored the goal which would take United to Wembley for the first time in 25 years, but sadly it wasn't to be.

We played the replay at Nottingham Forest and again drew 0-0. I had an exceptionally good game that day. Cup matches never went to penalties in those days, you just kept playing and playing until someone won, so off we went to Birmingham City's ground for the third game. In the first-half, Leicester won a penalty, which I saved. We then were awarded a penalty in the second-half, which was taken and missed by Graham Shaw. Leicester's Kenneth Leek scored the winner after we made a mistake at the back. We played in three games and could have won the tie, but we lost. I have to say that they were three great games and every ground we played at was absolutely packed.

After losing in a semi-final, it really hits you a few days later that you've missed out on going to Wembley. Hopefully, one day before I go to the great goalkeeper-maker in the sky, I can see Sheffield United play in a Cup Final at the new Wembley Stadium.

1960/61 was an outstanding season because we won promotion, finishing second behind Ipswich Town, who went on to win the First Division title the following season. Winning promotion back to the top flight was very important, of course, but ultimately the real glory prize was winning the FA Cup in those days, so we were desperately disappointed to have missed out on an appearance in the Final.

Although there was great rivalry between United and Wednesday, both sets of supporters could walk down The Moor in the centre of Sheffield with no confrontations. It was all great sporting banter. It was also like that with the players. We liked each other's company and would mix together after the games. There would be a fracas on the pitch at times with certain players. Sheffield Wednesday's Norman Curtis, for example, was a very hard man who would dish it out. But, although the matches were highly competitive, off the field we were great chums and I was proud of that; it's something I will always cherish. Wednesday goalkeeper Ron Springett and I were great friends. We went to the 1962 World Cup together in Chile and had a great camaraderie.

When we got relegated in the 1967/68 season, the United board thought they needed someone who was a bit harder and could manage the new players who were coming in, so Arthur Rowley was appointed. Unfortunately, it didn't work out, so John Harris returned as manager. The likes of Tony Currie, Len Badger, Alan Woodward, Mick Jones and Alan Birchenall emerged at that time. Tony was of course a great talent with a great football brain. Len was a very, very good player. He was a good passer of a ball who was highly rated around the country. He played a lot of youth international football and if he'd been at a bigger club, he'd have probably won a full cap. I'm not saying that Sheffield United is not a big club, but at that time we had a three-sided ground, so it never quite had the attraction of places like Highbury, Stamford Bridge or Anfield.

'Woody' was a great player and again, if he'd been at a bigger club, like Manchester United, Arsenal or Chelsea, I'm sure he would have been a regular international player. But he was quite happy to stay at Sheffield United, like we all were. In those days, there was a word called 'loyalty'. I know quite a bit about loyalty after playing for United for all those years, but I'm afraid in today's football, loyalty is a secondary consideration. Loyalty has been replaced by money. Players think, "Can I move and make money?" In those days we had loyalty because everyone was on the same money and everyone was playing for each other. Today, if a player doesn't like a club or falls out with the manager, he'll refuse to sign a new contract and look to move on. The situation will drag on until he gets a move. The boy Ashley Cole is a typical example.

After my playing career came to an end in the 1970/71 season, I took over the running of the United reserve team and did that for four years, taking my time with the club to 22 years. I then moved to Gillingham as assistant-manager, working under my old United team-mate Gerry Summers. I started doing some work for the FA, coaching goalkeepers. In fact I was the first-ever goalkeeping coach in the modern sense of the word, meaning a specialist coach for the keepers only. I was involved with the England youth team and told the FA that every team must have a goalkeeping coach.

After six years at Gillingham, the usual thing happened and I lost my job after we failed to get promotion. I'd been doing all these courses and decided to set up on my own as a coach, rather than being employed by one club, so I wrote off to managers up and down the country and found myself inundated with offers. There weren't enough days in the week to allow me to go round all the clubs who wanted me. I was then invited to go up to Scotland to do a course for them and I spent a week up there, working with about 18 goalkeepers. The Scottish FA were taken aback with the course I ran and I was working at Leicester one day when the new Scotland manager, Andy Roxburgh, rang me and asked if I'd become the goalkeeping coach for the national team. I accepted the offer without hesitation and started working with the goalkeepers, changing everything about their techniques. It was a good time to get involved with Scotland because Scottish goalkeepers were getting a lot of criticism from Jimmy Greaves on the *Saint & Greavsie* TV programme. I was with Scotland from 1986 until 2002 and it was a great time for me as I was involved in two World Cups and two European Championships. I also worked at Glasgow Rangers at the same time as coaching the national side.

I had a quadruple heart bypass operation 12 years ago. I was working at Rangers and thought I'd got 'flu. I flew back home feeling unwell and underwent surgery six days later. Within four weeks of the operation, I was out in Russia with the Scotland squad.

Another club I worked at was Manchester United and when I was there, Alex Ferguson sent me to watch a goalkeeper called Peter Schmeichel playing for Brondby in Denmark. United hadn't yet won the championship under Alex, so he was hanging on to his job. After watching Schmeichel, I came back and did a report. "This guy will win you the championship," I wrote. Alex signed him for £650,000, which was a bargain because he was absolutely superb. Schmeichel wasn't the finished article when he came to Old Trafford. I worked hard with him and changed him a helluva lot, but he did help Alex lift the title – several times!

Technically, I'd rate Andy Goram as probably the best goalkeeper I've ever worked with. I first met him when he was a young lad at Oldham and later worked with him at Rangers and with the Scotland squad. The only thing Schmeichel had over Goram was his height because Andy was a small goalie for the modern era.

After two years at Coventry City, I had a season at Rushden & Diamonds. I then went with the manager at Nene Park, Brian Talbot, when he moved on to Oxford, which is only 40 minutes from where I live in Rugby, and stayed at the club when Jim Smith took over in March 2006. I've known Jim since when he was a young lad at Bramall Lane. I'm a modern-day coach and I don't look back and say, "We did this and it was better in my day." I often compare football to long-distance running events. All the top records are going year after year in athletics. How the times have improved for the mile, for example, which is being run well under four minutes now, since Roger Bannister first ducked under that time while I was making my way as a young keeper at Bramall Lane. Football has also got faster over the years.

Unfortunately, we've lost our identity with all the foreign players in the English game. I look at my time at Manchester United when English players like David Beckham, Paul Scholes, Nicky Butt and the Neville brothers came through the ranks. That's no longer the case there; even the kids are foreign. At the highest level in this country, if three out of a 22-man squad are English, you're very, very lucky and that saddens me. There were some very good English goalies in the Seventies, Eighties and Nineties like Shilton, Clemence, Corrigan, Woods and Seaman. Unfortunately, there's a lack of good ones now due to the number of imports.

I've had a fabulous career and somebody, some day, may say, "Well done, Alan." I've been to two World Cups with England and two with Scotland, along with two European Championships. I've also been involved in over 200 internationals with Scotland. The 2006/07 season is my 54th season in the game and April 2007 marks fifty years since I made my first appearance for England. It was against Scotland at Wembley in front of a 100,000 crowd. I never dreamed that one day I'd be working for the Scottish national team as a coach. Stanley Matthews played in that game at the age of 45. The England side also included Tom Finney, Billy Wright, Duncan Edwards and Roger Byrne. I've still got the programme, which was autographed by every player.

The key to longevity is enjoying what you're doing. To mark my 70th birthday, I had a presentation at Oxford. When I gave a speech, I said, "It's not how you feel, it's how you enjoy the work you're doing." I've looked after myself and still do all the warm-ups and kick balls about with the goal-keepers I coach.

I get stacks of mail to my home and to the football club asking me to sign pictures from my playing days. I'll always cherish the United supporters because they were super and it was an honour to have played in front of them. They were great years to be playing. Now, it's more of a business. I've seen all the changes during my time in the game, with things like the foreign imports and the high wages being paid. Times have changed. Whether it's for the better, I don't know.

LEN BADGER
DEFENDER 1962–1976

BORN   8 June 1945, Sheffield
SIGNED   August 1962 from Apprentice
BLADES CAREER   512 games, 7 goals
HONOURS   Promotion from Division Two 1970/71, 13 England Under 23 caps
LEFT   Transferred to Chesterfield, January 1976; £3,000

A classy full-back who was a stalwart of the United side for a decade after coming through the ranks. He posed an attacking threat with purposeful runs down the right wing, linking up impressively with Alan Woodward. Len, who featured in the initial 40-man squad for the 1966 World Cup, was unlucky to miss out on a full England cap after representing his country at every other level

Sheffield United 5 v Cardiff City 1

League Division Two
Tuesday 27 April 1971

Bramall Lane
Attendance 42,963

*United thrash close rivals Cardiff to virtually seal promotion
to the First Division*

Teams

	Managers	
John Harris		Jimmy Scoular
Alan Hodgkinson	1	James Eadie
Len Badger	2	David Carver
Ted Hemsley	3	Gary Bell
John Flynn	4	Mel Sutton
Eddie Colquhoun	5	Don Murray
Trevor Hockey	6	Steve Derrett
Alan Woodward	7	Ian Gibson
Geoff Salmons	8	Brian Clark
Bill Dearden	9	Leighton Phillips
		(Sub. Robert Woodruff)
Tony Currie	10	Alan Warboys
Gil Reece	11	Peter King

	Scorers	
Dearden 6, 81, Flynn 33, Currie 55, Reece 66		Derrett 38

Referee: F Nicholson

I WAS AN England Schoolboy international and there were a lot of clubs who wanted to sign me as a teenager, including Manchester United and Tottenham, but I only ever wanted to go to Bramall Lane. I was brought up in the Tinsley area of Sheffield. My father died when I was ten, which made things tough for my mother, but I have only happy memories of my childhood. My family were Unitedites and I wouldn't have gone anywhere else. I would have walked on my hands to sign for United. I went to matches from being a young kid and Jimmy Hagan was my hero.

A United scout called Ernest Stevens came to our house to arrange for me to sign. John Harris was the manager at that time, with Archie Clark as his assistant. Archie was a good talent-spotter and a good second in command, who was totally different from John Harris. Whereas John was tee-total and a church-goer, Archie was a Scot who drank and swore. It was a good balance between them. Archie perhaps didn't get the recognition he deserved because he did a cracking job and brought a lot of players to the club.

I made my first appearance against Edmonton City, during a pre-season tour of Canada before the 1962/63 campaign. My first competitive appearance was against Bury in the League Cup in October 1962. We lost 3-1 with 'Doc' Pace, God bless him, scoring our goal. I made my league debut at home to Leyton Orient later in the season, shortly after helping the England Youth team win the junior World Cup. We beat Northern Ireland 4-1 at Wembley with a side which included future First Division stars Bernard Shaw, Ron Harris, Tommy Smith and John Sissons.

John Harris rewarded Bernard and I with call-ups to the first-team. After making a handful of appearances the following term, I established myself as a first-team regular in the 1964/65 season. We were in the First Division and I was playing for the club I wanted to play for. What could have been better? I think you're quite lucky in life if you end up doing something you want to do.

Alan Birchenall got into the side at the same time. 'Birch' came from Nottingham and he lived with me and my mother for six years before he was transferred to Chelsea. I think my mother thought more of him than she did of me! Birch was a proper lad and he still is. If you went anywhere in the world and put him with anyone – no matter who they were – he would take over because he's that strong a personality. I was the Best Man at his wedding. We ring each other periodically and he came to my mum's funeral recently.

John Harris handed the captaincy to me in 1965, which was a tremendous honour. Unfortunately, I had the great distinction of taking us down three years later! After finishing ninth and then sixth in Division Two, there were high hopes that we would win promotion in the 1970/71 season.

A 2-2 draw at QPR in mid-March was the start of a 11-match unbeaten run as we pushed hard for one of the two promotion places available then.

At the end of April, we faced a crucial game at home to Cardiff. We were in second place behind Leicester going into the game, just a point above Cardiff and having played a game more than them. Cardiff manager Jimmy Scoular said before the match that they needed to pick up at least a point. The pressure was on and the atmosphere was electric, with a crowd of just under 43,000 lighting up the Lane.

Billy Dearden gave us the lead after just six minutes. Either Billy or I could have scored that goal. After we were awarded a free-kick, Trevor Hockey played a ball behind the Cardiff wall and both Billy and I went through. I was very close to Billy when he stuck it away. Billy had so much courage and that's why he's in the state he's in now. Billy's had a big operation on his knee and he's in a right tangle. I see him quite often because he comes to my pub. Hockey was only 5ft 6ins tall, but he was a hard lad whose father was a Rugby League player from Keighley. If you were playing away from home and somebody was doing you a bit of damage, you could just say, 'Hock' and he'd do a job on them. He was a real character who stood out. When we signed him from Birmingham, he arrived in a Triumph Vitesse, which was a nice car, the difference being that he'd had it covered in velvet! It was fantastic.

Our second goal came on 33 minutes. Tony Currie took a free-kick from the left, I knocked the ball on at the near post and John Flynn met it with a diving header. If I shut my eyes, I can still picture it now. John, who I still see from time to time, was a quiet lad. He lives at Dinnington and works in the probation service over in Worksop. That was a cracking header and really put us in the driving seat.

Cardiff pulled a goal back in the 38th minute following a mistake from Ted Hemsley when Steve Derrett's effort took a deflection off Trevor

Hockey. It was a good balance with me and Ted on opposite sides of defence. I was the one who probably made all the forward runs while Ted steadied the ship at the back. He read the game well, which allowed me to do a little bit more going forward, taking a few chances.

Our goalkeeper, John Hope, was struggling after receiving a whack from one of the Cardiff forwards, Alan Warboys or Brian Clark, just before half-time. There was a bit of a scramble in the area and a Cardiff boot missed the ball, whacking John straight in the face. His face was covered in blood, but he carried on. John had taken over from Alan Hodgkinson, who was obviously a Blades legend. 'Hodgy' was 5ft 8ins tall, whereas 'Hopey' was 6ft 4ins. Hodgy was a great shot-stopper, but you couldn't expect him to come and get balls crossed into the box. 'Hopey' would come and get the ball and I think that helped us out towards the run-in because it gave you a bit of confidence. If you were confident of him getting the ball, you'd already be off and running, waiting for it to be thrown out.

The goal lifted Cardiff, who had a lot of possession in the second-half. But a 55th minute goal from Tony Currie eased the pressure. TC, who was of course a highly influential player for us, met an Alan Woodward corner with a header at the Bramall Lane end. Then Gil Reece made it 4-1 after 66 minutes with an unstoppable shot after Woody headed on a clearance from Carver. I know I'm biased, but Woody was special. He could score from 30 yards, take it round the keeper or chip him; he could do everything. He was the most under-estimated player. It makes you think what he should have had out of the game and won honours-wise. I had a telepathic understanding with Woody, which is one of those things you can't really explain. I knew that in his head was the same picture that I'd got in mine. I'd play a ball over the top and he knew what I was going to do. A lad called Steve Cammack played a few games for United and he was a good player, but we had different pictures in our heads. When I pictured playing the ball over the top, Cammy would instead come close. Me and Woody just knew instinctively what we were going to do.

Eddie Colquhoun was dominant in the air that day as usual. He was a no-nonsense centre-half who knew what he could do and what he couldn't do. Eddie was extremely quick for a big fella. He was a dour Scot, who appreciated his background because he wasn't the first to get a round in at the bar! Also playing that day was Geoff Salmons. 'Sammy' was a natural athlete who worked down the pit as a young lad for a while with his father before he came to Bramall Lane. He had a great left foot.

For me, a footballer's biggest high comes when you play in a game like that. The pitch is a bit greasy and it's night time, so it's dark and there's nothing to distract you, making concentration levels higher than normal. When you come off and you've won like we did, you get in the bath and you'll never be as high as that again in your life, no matter what you do. That's what happens to professional footballers; when they finish, they go on trying to find that high. I've never, ever succeeded in doing that. Try alcohol, try anything you want, but it never gives you that.

We were so elated after the match and we went for a drink at the Penny Farthing nightclub, which was at the back of The Moor in the centre of Sheffield. By the time quarter-to-one came round, everybody began to think about the next game. There were about eight or nine of us there and it suddenly dawned on us that promotion hadn't yet been achieved. We knew we had to get at least a point at the weekend. Suddenly there we were thinking, "We've got to do it all again on Saturday."

The club was absolutely buzzing at that time and we socialised together a lot. Sometimes we'd all go out with our wives, but Monday night was always a lads' night out. We'd be in the dressing room and one of the lads would say, "Somebody pick a pub to go to tonight." It wasn't just the first-team going out, there would be all sorts of people from the club, so there might be 20-30 out. The celebrations after Cardiff strengthened our resolve rather than deadened our spirit and we beat Watford 3-0 at the weekend to secure promotion. Stuart Scullion hit the crossbar for Watford and Keith Eddy gave a penalty away. I don't know whether it was a coincidence, but they both later signed for us! We celebrated by going to the Fiesta club.

I remember watching Yorkshire play Worcestershire at Bramall Lane in the summer. Ted Hemsley was playing for Worcestershire and I was in the cricket pavilion with Ted when the United secretary, Arnold Newton, came in and told us the fixture list was out for the forthcoming season. We looked at the games and saw we faced Southampton, Leeds, Everton, Arsenal and West Brom at the start of the season. There were only two points for a win then and we said, "To get two points out of that would be fantastic."

We hammered Southampton and Leeds. Then we went to Everton and won 1-0 before the big one at Highbury. Arsenal had just done the League and Cup double and we beat them. We were playing some fantastic stuff and absolutely flying. Players were knocking the ball about and going round people; TC was dropping his shoulder and blowing kisses to the crowd. We had the right balance and played with no fear. It was the same home or away, with everybody fitting into the system. We drew 0-0 against

West Brom before beating Huddersfield and Nottingham Forest. We got beat 2-0 at Manchester United, but the scoreline doesn't tell the whole story because we played quite well and could have been a couple of goals up. But Ted Hemsley got injured and that contributed to the special goal scored by George Best, which is regularly shown on TV. Gil Reece came on and played at left-back. Besty picked the ball up and Gil stayed too close to Trevor Hockey. If Ted had been playing he wouldn't have done that; he'd have stayed off and forced him wide. If you watch the goal on TV, I end up in the back of the net. No matter how many times I look at it, I never get any closer to keeping the ball out! They were refurbishing Old Trafford, limiting the crowd to around 50,000, so there were about 20,000 locked out that night. Even so, when they scored, the roar from the crowd was absolutely deafening.

Ken Furphy was appointed manager and he was totally different from the man he replaced, John Harris. He was a bit go-ahead and a bit flash. He'd been manager of Blackburn and he signed Third Division players like Tony Field, Terry Garbett and Terry Nicholl to come and play in the First Division. They were good, honest professionals, but they didn't have the quality. We just missed out on Europe in Furphy's first season. We needed two points at Birmingham and we ended up drawing after Tony Currie missed a sitter. He went round three people and side-footed the ball past the post. It was late on in the game and if that had gone in, we'd have been playing in Europe. I'll never forgive TC for denying me the chance to play in Europe!

We finished sixth, but we won so many games we didn't deserve to win. It was one of those freaks. The writing was on the wall because we were getting away with bloody murder. That proved to be the case the following season. Jimmy Sirrell came in to replace Furphy and he was a good, honest man, but there was something missing. Sirrell wanted big, strong types who could whack it up and get up and down the pitch. When Sirrell dropped me, he said, "Aye son, you're no big enough to play at the back."

"Well Jim, I'm 31, I don't think I'm going to grow any more," I replied.

"Find yourself another club, son."

I had 18 months left on my contract, but I left straight away because I always make wrong decisions. I should have stayed really because that's where my heart was. I don't know whether I'd have got back in the side as I think Jimmy had made his mind up. That's fair enough because every manager his own way of playing and I had no divine right to be there. I'm fairly placid, but then my sense goes and everything else goes completely. The only problem was my bloody ego. I should have stayed because I was at a place I loved. Why shouldn't I have played in the reserves? I had no right to expect to play in the first-team, but that was what I thought at the time.

I sorted myself out because the legendary Joe Shaw, who lived next door to me, was the manager of Chesterfield and he took me to Saltergate. After spending 16 years at Bramall Lane, I assumed United would let me go for nothing. But I was told that they wanted a fee for me, which I couldn't believe. I said, "Come on, my mother's put every kid up who's ever come to Bramall Lane for nothing and looked after everybody." When they still insisted on a fee, I told them where to go and stormed off. That's a big regret of mine because I shouldn't have done that.

United did receive a fee for me from Chesterfield, so I never got anything. But the people of Sheffield rewarded me because I had a good testimonial with a crowd of 23,000, which was fantastic. I was only at Chesterfield for two-and-a-half years. I made 46 appearances and broke my leg twice while I was there. I remember as a kid talking to former United player Harry Latham, who was a trainer at the club, asking him when you knew it was time to finish playing. "Don't worry son, you'll know," he replied. When I broke my leg the first time, it never entered my head to finish playing. Arthur Cox, who had come in as manager, got me the fittest I'd been. After playing in a few reserve games, I made my first-team comeback against Tranmere at Saltergate. I'd not really tested the leg until that point, so I went in for a hard challenge and heard the bone snap. I could see Harry's face and I thought, "I know now, Harry, don't you worry." I realised it was time to go.

In our day, you knew that you weren't going to be financially sound from playing football. You knew you had to do something else once you finished playing. I was in business at the time with a paper manufacturing company, which was going quite well, so I had to make the decision whether to cling on to football or concentrate on the business. My daughter was being educated and I didn't want to drag her up to Darlington or wherever, so I made the decision to stay out of the game. I moved into the pub trade in 1980, starting off in partnership with someone at The Sidings in Dronfield. We also had a wine bar in Dronfield called Ferkins. Then I was at The Peacock in Barlow for ten years and also worked in advertising at Sheffield Newspapers for a while. I've been at The Fox and Goose pub in Chesterfield since 1990.

When I reflect on my career, it's a total and utter regret that I didn't win a full England cap, but you can't change it, can you? It's done and dusted. I only have myself to blame because I played for England Schoolboys, then the youth side and Under-23s. I also played for the Football League side. There was a Football League game in Belgium after the 1966 World Cup and it was quite an honour to play for the Football League. It was virtually the World Cup side, with me playing in place of George Cohen. I pinged in a cross in for a young Allan Clarke to score at the near post and we won 2-1. I went out in Brussels with players like Bobby Moore, Alan Ball and Martin Peters. Of course, everywhere we went, everybody knew who they were. When it came to me, they were like, "Len Badger?" We got absolutely arse-holed. I was that pissed, I had to crawl along the corridor to find my hotel room. I found the room and started kicking the door, trying to attract the attention of my room-mate Norman Hunter. I looked up from my position on the floor as the door opened and stood there was Alf Ramsey, who wasn't best pleased. I don't know whether that had any bearing on my international career, but nothing else happened after that.

I had been in the initial 40-man squad for the 1966 World Cup before it was whittled down. I think things would have been different if I'd had a bit more sense. I could have made more of it, but that's what I was as a person and I'm probably as stupid now. It's down to realizing your opportunities when they arise. I trained hard, but there are certain times in your life when opportunities arise and I didn't take full advantage. Looking back, I suppose I was fairly immature, but fairly honest in what I was doing.

Sadly, two of the players who played in that game against Cardiff, Trevor Hockey and Gil Reece, have passed away. Trevor was a nice man, God bless him. He played in TC's testimonial at Bramall Lane in 1986 when we had the promotion-winning side playing against Dennis Waterman's All Star XI. I hadn't seen Hock for maybe ten years, but it was just like old times. A few weeks later, he was coaching kids when he collapsed and died after bending down to tie his laces. He was the fittest man, who ran all day, so it just shows you. Gil died a couple of years ago.

It was a tragic story because he had a cyst on his knee, which they kept trying to sort out. He had a number of operations and eventually had to have his leg off. I went down with Ted Hemsley and Geoff Salmons to see him at his hotel in Cardiff. Reecey had got his false leg on and when he came over, I said, "Bloody hell, Gilbert. You ought to have worn that when you were playing, you've sent me four ways already!" That was the sort of humour we enjoyed when we were playing. We had a fantastic day with him, sat on a veranda in Tiger Bay, just drinking and reminiscing. We phoned everybody up we could think of and then went home and that's the last time I saw him. All the boys from the team went down to his funeral. Gil played for Cardiff after leaving United and all the boys from that team were there as well. The funeral was on a Friday and the ironic thing was that United were playing Cardiff at Ninian Park the following day.

I often go to United's midweek matches and sometimes on a Saturday, if I can. It would be great if they could stay up in the top flight and maybe consolidate. The ground is fantastic now and the club is in good order because the chairman seems to be quite a wise man, who's got things sorted off the pitch.

For my 50th birthday, Ted Hemsley and Tony Currie bought me a great big painting of Bramall Lane as it used to be. I see Ted every week and I play golf with TC most Thursdays, mainly in the winter, at Worksop. Colin Franks came over from Canada last year and we got all the lads together for a drink. We also meet up when Woody comes over from the United States, but he's not been back for about 18 months.

With the wages we earned in our day, we were closer to the fans. We lived in the same areas, whereas today's players don't live in the areas where the majority of the supporters live, so they have isolated existences. I'd liked to have had the money they earn today because everybody would, but I'm glad that I played in an era when the relationship between the players and fans was fairly close. It meant more to me playing for United because I was a Sheffield lad. It was my life and I loved it.

TONY CURRIE
MIDFIELDER 1968-1976

BORN   1 January 1950, Edgware, London
SIGNED   February 1968 from Watford; £26,500
BLADES CAREER   346 games, 59 goals
HONOURS   Promotion from Division Two 1970/71, 17 England caps,
13 England U23 caps
LEFT   Transferred to Leeds United, June 1976; £245,00

A supremely gifted midfielder, who is widely regarded as one of United's greatest-ever players, Currie combined superb passing and excellent close control with powerful and accurate shooting, making him a much feared opponent. With his flamboyant style, often blowing kisses to the fans during games, Tony was a real crowd-pleaser. He has spent nearly 20 years as United's Football In The Community Officer.

Sheffield United 3 v West Ham United 2

League Division One
Saturday 22 March 1975

Bramall Lane
Attendance 25,527

A sparkling two-goal display from Currie sees the Blades twice come
from behind to beat the Hammers in a thrilling match

Teams

Ken Furphy	**Managers**	John Lyall
Jim Brown	1	Mervyn Day
Len Badger	2	Keith Coleman
David Bradford	3	Frank Lampard
Keith Eddy	4	John McDowell
Eddie Colquhoun	5	Tommy Taylor
John Flynn	6	Kevin Lock
Alan Woodward	7	Billy Jennings
Mick Speight	8	Graham Paddon
Steve Cammack	9	Alan Taylor
Tony Currie	10	Trevor Brooking
Tony Field	11	Bobby Gould

Currie 9, 79, Woodward 57	**Scorers**	Gould 8, Jennings 29

Referee: J Taylor

SHEFFIELD UNITED MANAGER John Harris came down to Watford with a scout to look at winger Stewart Scullion and ended up signing me. Watford needed to sell somebody for a substantial fee to renew the lease on the ground and £26,500 for me was quite a bit of money in those days. Scullion ended up coming to Bramall Lane a few years later.

I was a striker when United signed me and I'd scored quite a few goals in the youth team and reserves at Vicarage Road. I made the headlines by scoring nine goals in my first six games for Watford's first team and scored my first hat-trick in only my third game. In my first season with United, 1967/68, I only scored four goals in 13 games and unfortunately we went down to the Second Division. The following season, I only scored five goals in 48 appearances and that's awful for a striker, but I probably made most of the goals for the team. During the close-season, I had a chat with John Harris and told him I thought I might be better off making goals. "I'd like to play in midfield because I'm coming back and making goals for everybody else," I said. He agreed to give it a try and a couple of years later, I was playing in England's midfield.

John Harris was like a quiet Bill Shankly. He could have been Shankly's brother because they were both tough Scots. But the difference was that John was a very private gentleman who never drank or smoked and he didn't like the limelight at all. He didn't want to talk to the Press and he didn't even talk much in team meetings, leaving it more to the players. Alf Ramsey was a bit like that as well. John was always in a collar and tie, never in a tracksuit. He'd be there for every training session, walking about and observing, but he left the training to John Short who was the first-team coach. Cec Coldwell later took over the role of coach. Harris became General Manager following relegation from the First Division and Arthur Rowley came in as team manager. Arthur was also quiet, but he was different to John because he was brash. He instilled confidence in you and I got on with him well, but he perhaps just didn't get the right team together or play the right tactics. We had a good team, but we didn't have a good squad, so we struggled if anyone got injured.

After Arthur was given the bullet, the manager's job was given back to John Harris. We finished sixth in the 1969/70 season, which was the only year that Sheffield Wednesday were in the same league as us during my time with United, so I only played in two derby games in my nine years at the club. I was voted Player of the Year at the end of the 1970/71 campaign as we won promotion, finishing second behind Leicester. We finished tenth the following season after taking the First Division by storm. We were at the top of the table after an unbeaten ten-match run at the start of the season, which included winning our first four away matches against Arsenal, Everton, Nottingham Forest and Fulham. In our 11th match, we were beaten by Manchester United at Old Trafford, with George Best scoring that goal they always show, where he beats almost the entire defence before slotting home. We'd have taken tenth place at the start of the season, but to be at the top of the League for a couple of months and then finish tenth was a bit sickening really.

Keith Eddy, who I'd played with at Watford, came in before the start of the 1972/73 season. Keith was a great player and I think if it hadn't been for Bobby Moore, he'd have played for England. He was such a good reader of the game and could pass a good ball. He was also calm and collected and a great penalty-taker. Alan Woodward should also have played for England. The fact that he didn't was just down to the fact that he was at United. If you played for a big club or one of the London clubs, you got picked. We were seen as an unfashionable club. Woody should have had a few caps at least. He was a phenomenal player who scored goals as a winger. He was a top-class finisher who hit the ball powerfully with his left or right foot and was great at dead-balls. Len Badger was another fella who should have made it at international level. He had loads of talent as a ball-playing full-back.

After finishing 14th in the 1972/73 season, we ended the following term a place higher. It was in the early part of that season when I famously sat on the ball during our 5-0 win over Arsenal at Bramall Lane. When Arsenal had absolutely stuffed us 5-0 at The Lane in 1972, Alan Ball just stopped and sat on the ball when I went to challenge him. Bally and I were good pals because he'd taken me under his wing for England and we're still great friends now. I could have gone and kicked the ball from under him or what-ever, but I didn't. I just stood there and clapped. Two years later, the scores were reversed when we were leading 4-0 and I'd scored two goals in the first-half, so it was just my chance to get my own back. The thing is that he did it on the half-way line and I did it in our box. When I got up, I tripped over the ball and they nearly scored from it! Bally came up to me after the match and said, "Nice one, I'll have one for you next time." He did because next time we played he put his foot on the ball and pretended to tie his laces. You wouldn't get away with those sort of antics nowadays.

Ken Furphy, who replaced John Harris as manager in December 1973, was an arrogant man, certainly to me. When I was at Watford, he said in the papers that he'd given me my chance and that he wouldn't be playing me if I wasn't scoring goals. He thought I was lazy as a young player. Perhaps it was me being young and naïve, but I was learning the game and thought I was doing okay. I used to get people calling me lazy, but I've got videos showing me winning the ball and then finishing moves off quite a few times, so I don't think I was.

When I was reunited with Furphy five years after leaving Watford, I didn't feel that I had anything to prove to him because by now I was an England international at the top of my game. He did try to put me down a few times, why I don't know, perhaps because I was idolised and he wanted to be. He brought in players who'd been with him at Blackburn: Terry Garbett, Tony Field and David Bradford. I felt it was a bit like Cloughie doing what he did at Leeds and Furphy upset some of our players because there was a bit of a clique with him and those three players. Garbett and Bradford were great lads, but Tony Field was a bit difficult to take because he had an attitude. He was quite a skilful lad, but perhaps not a team player.

I signed a six-year contract in the 1973/74 season to take me up to 1980. I've never revealed this before, but the main reason I signed the contract was to put an end to speculation about my future because I didn't want to leave. Manchester United manager Tommy Docherty wanted me at the time to replace Bobby Charlton and I was receiving phone calls at home from Old Trafford representatives. Of course you're tempted when a big club like that comes in for you, but I didn't like change and I was very happy where I was. Perhaps I was wrong, maybe I should have gone to Manchester United and replaced Charlton.

It was a difficult time at Bramall Lane because the building of the new South Stand, which took two years, meant there was little available cash to spend in the transfer market. Even so, we felt that we had a genuine chance of qualifying for Europe in the 1974/75 season, especially after making a good start to the season. One blip early on came when we lost 5-1 at Leeds. We were always liable to do that because we were an attacking team, first and foremost. It was very difficult for us to play defensively with the players we had in the team, so it was always a good match to watch, whoever we played.

We went into the West Ham game with our hopes of qualifying for Europe still very much alive after suffering just one defeat in our previous ten league games. There were a number of landmarks that day, starting with the fact that car dealership Gilders became the first-ever sponsors of a United game. On a personal note, I was making my 300th League and Cup appearance for the club. Billy Dearden missed the game after being injured the previous week when we played well in a goal-less draw at Liverpool. Steve Cammack came into the attack as Billy's replacement.

West Ham, who were missing their skipper Billy Bonds, took an eighth-minute lead when Bobby Gould scored from close-range after meeting a cross from John McDowell. I equalised just a minute later after starting and finishing the move. I played the ball over from the left-wing to Alan Woodward who saw his shot blocked, then Steve Cammack's follow up hit the post and as the ball came across the line, I tapped it in from about six inches. It was my 50th league goal for United, so it was a bit special.

West Ham regained the lead following a mistake from Jim Brown. Billy Jennings tried a speculative overhead kick and Jim made a hash of trying to catch the ball because it went over his shoulder and into the net. It looked horrible. He made a couple of mistakes, but everybody does. Jim was a very good keeper.

After finding ourselves 2-1 down at half-time, we drew level again 12 minutes into the second-half following a goal from Alan Woodward. Brown threw the ball out to Cammack on the right and he passed to 'Woody' who controlled the ball with his left foot before firing home with his right. That goal was another landmark because it was the 1,000th scored by United in the First Division in post-war years.

I then hit the bar and so did Cammack before my individual goal in the 79th minute which proved to be the winner. It started off with me winning the ball in a tackle about ten yards inside our own half. Everybody says I never used to tackle, but I've got video evidence to prove it! I block-tackled somebody right on the byline and the ball went to Cammack who played it to Woodward. Woody then played it back to me after I'd crept up to the half-way line. By the time I got up to the box, I was swaying this way and that before placing a left-foot shot into the corner of the net. It looked like keeper Mervyn Day was stuck to the ground because he didn't move. Although it was a bit of a zig-zag manoeuvre at the end of it, I didn't actually beat any players. Lots of people thought I'd beaten three or four players, but that wasn't the case. Kevin Lock just kept backing off and taking my dummies and I kept going back onto the other foot. The goal has been shown many times on TV because the game was featured on Match of the Day. It was lucky because we rarely featured on Match of the Day. It was usually the big boys who were shown and we had to settle for appearing on Yorkshire TV on their Sunday programme. In his commentary, John Motson famously described it as "a quality goal from a quality player". I thanked him many years later when I met him in a pub in Hertfordshire. I was out with some friends when I saw him and we had a little chat about the game. Everybody thinks that was my best goal. It's probably my most memorable one because people always talk about it.

Just a minute after the goal, I was denied a hat-trick when Mervyn Day did well to turn my effort over the bar. You get those days where you get lots of the ball and have plenty of shots and there are other times when you don't. Len Badger became the third United player to hit the bar at the Kop end while West Ham still looked threatening when they went forward and Brown had to make a couple of good saves from Gould. We were similar teams and it was always a good, open game between us. The fans certainly got their money's worth that day. As we walked off the pitch at the end of the game, the PA announcer played 'You Can Do Magic' by Limmie and the Family Cookin', which became something of a signature tune for me. When I hear the song, it always brings back great memories. It's an unbelievable high when you've performed like that and you can never replace the buzz you got from playing football. Just to be out there, showing 20,000-30,000 people what you can do, especially when you've won. I used to blow kisses to the crowd. I could hear everything the fans were saying to me and I always had a bit of banter with them. I think that's what they enjoyed. It was a fantastic time because we were a great team of friends and all got on fantastically well.

Teams would often stick somebody on me to try and cut out the supply to our forward line. It's very difficult to shrug somebody off when they're just following you and have no interest in the game. Their job is just to follow you about to try and make sure you don't get a kick. I wanted to be the best player every time, but there's always the other team trying to stop you, no matter how. That's what happens, so it wasn't through want of trying that I didn't play to the best of my ability in every game. I was always self-critical because I'm a bit of a perfectionist, so I could be moody if I didn't have a good game. I felt I did pretty well percentage-wise in the 600-odd games I played in my career. There were also lots of times I was asked to play when I was probably only about 50-60 per cent fit and people didn't realise that.

I'd rate my performance against West Ham as being in my top three ever. It said in the match report in the Sheffield Star that it was a pity England manager Don Revie wasn't there to witness it. But it wouldn't have made any difference with Don because he didn't like flair players. He made it clear during an England get-together that players like myself, Stan Bowles, Alan Hudson, Rodney Marsh and Frank Worthington didn't figure in his plans. I suppose he thought we weren't team players. I won 17 caps from 1972 to 1979, including seven during my time at United, which wasn't a lot, but I missed out on three years really when Revie was in charge. He only played me once and he didn't really want to play me then, it was only because of pressure from the Press. But I got more caps than the likes of Bowles, Hudson, Marsh and Worthington. I also played 12 times at Wembley and there are lots of players who never played there at all.

We were in eighth place after beating West Ham, five points behind leaders Everton with a game in hand. We went on to narrowly miss out on a European spot, although we did have a big say in the title-race after destroying the hopes of both Everton and Stoke. We finished sixth, just four points behind champions Derby, so it was very close.

Chris Guthrie was brought in over the summer for around £100,000 and that proved to be a waste of money. He was very good in the air, but that was about it because he wasn't mobile. He certainly wasn't a Billy Dearden. After a poor start to the season, Jimmy Sirrell came in to replace Ken Furphy and I got on well with him. He'd had Don Masson at Notts County and he compared me to him. The only thing with Jimmy was that he loved practice matches, so we seemed to play them from Monday to Friday and then had to go out on Saturday and do the same thing. At the half-way stage, we created an unwanted new League record after picking up only five points. We were down by Christmas because we were that far away. We just got into a rut and couldn't get out of it. We were getting regular thrashings, it seemed almost weekly, and it was a very depressing time. My game was suffering as well. We finished bottom after winning just six games.

When I got back from the end of season tour to Gibraltar, Jimmy Sirrell said that John Harris wanted me to go to his house. When I got there, we just got in John's car and he started driving. I daren't ask him where we were going and he wasn't the sort of person who'd say anything. We drove up to Leeds and I still didn't know where we were going until we pulled in at Elland Road. I hadn't been tapped up by Leeds, so it was a total shock when

I found out that their manager, Jimmy Armfield, wanted to sign me. I'd put in three transfer requests that season, but they were all turned down. Interest from other clubs was shielded from me, so I never got to hear about it. A lot of people thought I deserted United, but I'd signed a six-year contract two years before I left and not many people sign a contract of that length. I'd have probably ended up signing another one after that, but we got relegated and I couldn't afford to stay any longer because I was an England international and I didn't want to lose that. I thought it was time to go after nine years at the club. You can't take a chance and think you're going to come straight back up again.

I fitted in straight away at Leeds, taking the place of Johnny Giles. I was a very similar player to him, spraying the ball about. There were a number of international players in the side who were still great players despite the fact they were getting on. I stayed at Leeds for three seasons and didn't want to leave there. It was just that my wife at the time wanted to go back to London, so I moved to QPR. Tommy Docherty was the manager who signed me (he finally got me after trying to sign me for Man United), but Terry Venables replaced him two years later. We got QPR to the 1982 FA Cup Final, a showpiece event which I thought had passed me by. Spurs did very well in the first game, but we kept in it and took them to a replay. I captained the side in the replay because Glenn Roeder was suspended. I was thinking, "This is it. This is my dream to be in a Cup Final at Wembley and winning the Cup." Being captain as well, I thought it was all set up for me to lift the Cup. But it wasn't in the end because we lost and I gave a bloody penalty away! I was tracking Graham Roberts from the half-way line and everybody seemed to be opening up, letting him go through and through and then when he was about to draw his foot back, I brought him down. I got a right roasting from Terry Venables a half-time. 'You shouldn't have dived in because Peter Hucker would have saved it,' he said.

Venables was great to play under because he was the best coach. He was a great tactician and could handle the players and deal with the Press. He's got all that plus a great knowledge of the game and should still be England manager. I was suffering injury problems by then. I'd had a cartilage out when I was 24 and by the time I was 29/30, the knee was starting to give me a few problems. Venables put an Astroturf pitch down at Loftus Road, which didn't do me any favours at all. It probably cut my career by about three or four years. In four years at QPR, I only made about 80 League appearances. I made just one appearance in my last season there because my knee was shot.

After a brief spell at Torquay, I ended up playing in non-league football in the south for Chesham, Hendon, Finchley and Dunstable. I basically played for anybody who wanted to give me a game. I'm the type who would have gone on and on because when I was 37, I ended up playing for Goole after moving back up north. I'd still be playing Sunday League football now if my left knee was as good as my right because you can't replace playing the game. I can't ride a bike or jog now because I'd be in a chair for three weeks.

It was a very difficult time for me after retiring from playing. I was living at home with my mum, because I'd got divorced a year after leaving Leeds, which was a big downer because I hadn't wanted to leave Elland Road after being very happy there. But things didn't work out with my wife, so we divorced. I wasn't living with my kids who were four miles away. I was left with hardly anything after the divorce settlement and from 1983 to 1988, I was just messing about, not doing much really. I had to look after my kids, so to make ends meet I did odd jobs here and there, including some mini-cabbing for a couple of months. I got offered the manager's job at Wigan by ex-Sheffield United director Tony Barrington in about 1984, but I turned it down. Wigan were in the lower divisions in those days, but it would have been a start. It's a big regret because I should have taken it. I would have been about 34 or 35 and who knows what would have happened. I could have ended up being England manager! You never know how things would have worked out and that's down to the fact that I didn't take the bloody chance. I applied for the Rotherham job before Ronnie Moore got it and I also applied for the job at Shrewsbury. But I didn't get an interview for either position. I also put in for the Sheffield United job twice – before Dave Bassett and after he was in charge – but that was only under pressure from friends. Fans were writing to the local paper saying I should be the manager, so I felt obliged to apply. I didn't expect to get it and perhaps didn't really want it, so I wasn't disappointed when I didn't get a reply.

I was granted a testimonial at Bramall Lane in 1986, so I came up for that and stayed up. I moved in with a lady I ended up marrying and then landed the Football In The Community job back at Sheffield United. It was a new initiative and I applied for the job and got it. Funnily enough, I started work on 1 February 1988, which was exactly 20 years to the day after I actually signed for United. I felt very fortunate to be getting up in the mornings and going to work at a club where I'd had such happy times. I've never grown up and I still feel 21, although I don't look it! I'm still Football In The

Community Officer at Bramall Lane. We coach kids in school time and after school and organise birthday parties nearly every night at the club because they're so popular. We also do soccer schools during every school holiday. We don't close down when the season ends because we're working all the time throughout the year.

Things are looking great for United. The stadium is first-class and there are so many more plans for things which haven't got off the ground yet. We're a big club and let's just hope we can prove it on the field. If we hadn't developed things like the academy, we probably wouldn't have achieved promotion. It's all part of the steps you have to take to get to the top. We trained at the Ball Inn training ground in my day, which consisted of a pitch, two small changing rooms and a couple of little showers. If the ball went over the top of net, it would run down to East Bank Road and it'd take you ten minutes to go and find it!

To be mentioned in the same breath as Jimmy Hagan when people talk about United's greatest-ever players is some tribute. Not that I ever saw Jimmy play, but it's what you hear from other people about how great he was. I've done some match day hospitality work at United and I also do the odd after-dinner engagement. I take my memorabilia with me and people love to see items like shirts and medals. When I get together with my old mates like Len Badger, Ted Hemsley and Alan Woodward, we often talk about the some of the games we played in. I've got a video of the West Ham game, which I've watched many times. I'll sometimes put it on if we have visitors and they want to see that goal again. It wasn't bad.

GARY HAMSON

MIDFIELDER 1976–1979

BORN   24 August 1959, Sandiacre
SIGNED   November 1976 from Apprentice
BLADES CAREER   116 games, 9 goals
LEFT   Transferred to Leeds United, July 1979; £140,000

An industrious left-sided midfielder who ensured his place in Blades folklore by scoring a memorable late winner against Liverpool when the Reds were at the peak of their powers. Gary made over 100 appearances for United while still a teenager. He was a fixture in the side before being transferred to Leeds, against his wishes, for a six-figure fee. Injuries blighted his career at Elland Road, preventing him from realising his true potential.

Sheffield United 1 v Liverpool 0

League Cup Second Round
Monday 28 August 1978

Bramall Lane
Attendance 35,753

The Blades stun mighty Liverpool, the reigning League and European champions, on an unforgettable night at 'Beautiful Downtown' Bramall Lane

Teams

Harry Haslam	**Managers**	Bob Paisley
Steve Conroy	1	Ray Clemence
John Cutbush	2	Phil Neal
Paul Garner	3	Alan Kennedy
Andy Keeley	4	Phil Thompson
John Matthews	5	Ray Kennedy
Mick Speight	6	Emlyn Hughes
Alan Woodward	7	Kenny Dalglish
Simon Stainrod	8	Jimmy Case
		(Sub. David Fairclough)
Steve Finnieston	9	Steve Heighway
(Sub. Colin Franks)		
Gary Hamson	10	Terry McDermott
Alex Sabella	11	Graeme Souness

Hamson 80	**Scorers**	

Referee: D Lloyd

As THE YEARS go by, people keep saying, "I was there, I remember you scoring against Liverpool" and it's what most people remember me for. In some ways that's sad because I never really fulfilled my potential due to injury problems, but you can never take that moment against Liverpool away from me.

I grew up supporting Nottingham Forest and looked set to join them after training with them as a kid. John McGovern and John O'Hare used to pick me up and take me to training. That carried on for a period of time and I was given the impression they were going to offer me an apprenticeship. But when it came to the time when a decision needed to be made, Brian Clough was away in Majorca. Alan Hill, who was Forest's chief scout, told my father that they were 90 per cent certain to take me on, but explained they had to wait until Clough came back.

In the meantime, I played in a representative youth match between teams from Nottinghamshire and Mansfield. I was playing for Ilkeston Town juniors at that time and was included in the Notts side. We won 4-1 and I scored a hat-trick from midfield. A Sheffield United scout called Neville Briggs, who had followed Jimmy Sirrell from Notts County to United, was watching the game. Briggs told Sirrell he'd seen me play and gave me a glowing report. That was on the Wednesday and on the Saturday, the United youth team were playing at West Brom in a friendly. They invited me to go and play for them and I accepted, so they picked me up at junction 25 of the M1, which was near where I lived. I had a really good game and the following day I signed as an apprentice, so they effectively pinched me from under Forest's nose.

As a Forest fan, I wanted to sign for them, but the decision was driven by my parents and I didn't have a say in the matter. My dad said, "Look, Cloughie might come back and not offer you an apprenticeship, so I'd sign for Sheffield United." I duly signed for Sheffield United, which meant that within less than a week, I'd been spotted by United, played a game for them and then signed, which was unbelievable. The move forced me to leave home at the age of 16 and I didn't go back because I married my wife when I was 18 or 19.

The young pros at United who'd already got into the first-team were John McGeady, Tony Kenworthy, Simon Stainrod and Keith Edwards. John and Keith were slightly older than Tony and Simon and I was the youngest of the bunch. The rest of them had been apprentices for probably a year when I came on the scene. We looked up to Alan Woodward because he was still acknowledged as the best player at the club at that time, despite the fact that he was in his thirties. There was also Ian 'Chico' Hamilton who was a flair player, Eddie Colquhoun was a good steady player at the back, Jim Brown was a really good goalkeeper and Ted Hemsley was coming towards the end of his career.

Legendary former Celtic winger Jimmy Johnstone was also there. He was a bit-part player because he was in his thirties when he came to Bramall Lane. But despite being in the twilight of his career and past his best, he was still unbelievable. When I played with him in the reserves, players could never get the ball off him. When people paid tribute to Jimmy following his death and said you couldn't get the ball off him, they weren't joking. If you wanted a rest, you would just have to ping the ball over to the right-wing and he'd keep it for 30 seconds or a minute, allowing you to have a breather. He'd go on a mazy run and keep the ball in the corner, taking the mickey and win you a throw in or put a cross over.

Talking of great players, I just missed Tony Currie twice in my career. When I joined Sheffield United, I missed him by a few months and when I moved to Leeds, he'd just gone to QPR. It was a shame that I never played with him because he's one of my favourite players.

My full debut came after United had been relegated from the First Division in 1975/76, away against Cardiff in October 1976 and we won 2-0. Simon Stainrod scored twice, but I received all the plaudits. I set up both goals and according to Tony Pritchett, who covered United for Sheffield newspaper The Star, I gave a "veteran's performance" as a 17 year-old in midfield. At that time, my game was all about passing and I also had a good engine. I got in the side and stayed in and when we played Cardiff in the return game in the New Year, I scored my first league goal. Jimmy Sirrell was a very good manager and he's someone I have a lot of respect for. He's a real football man who liked to try and educate you. He gave me my chance and I took it.

We were thrilled to get the chance to face Liverpool in the League Cup. In the build-up to the tie, new manager Harry Haslam told the Press that no-one in Great Britain gave us a chance of winning, adding that the role of underdog suited him. The match had caught the imagination of the fans and there were crowds of them queuing up to buy tickets. In the game before the Liverpool match, we drew 2-2 at Preston on the Saturday, with Argentinian midfielder Alex Sabella scoring his first goal for the club.

Sabella had been signed from River Plate for £160,000 in the summer, which was a record fee for United at that time. Alex was a fantastically gifted player, probably better than anyone I've ever played with, but he was a luxury in my opinion because he wasn't really a team player. His work ethic was poor and he wouldn't close players down, he'd just let them run past him. We played a 4-4-2 formation, with four midfielders against four midfielders, and what it basically meant was that when the opposition had the ball, it was like we were playing three against four. Alex would just be walking the other way and he'd only switch on when we had the ball. As soon as we were in possession, he'd be saying, "Give it me, give it me." It was a big point when it came to Alex's contribution that not a lot of people picked up on. I picked up on it, though, because I was doing his running! When he did have the ball at his feet, you'd be shouting, "Alex, I'm here, I'm here, give it me." But he often wouldn't give it to you until you were marked up.

Alex turned it on against Sunderland when we won 3-1 in front of the Match of the Day cameras, doing the beautiful skill on the byeline and pulling the ball back to Steve Finnieston who knocked it in. People remember that, but there was also the defeat at home to Millwall when Alex was a joke and never tracked back. They absolutely ran us into the ground because he had an off-day. Then he had another off-day and another off-day, but people would say, "Sabella had a brilliant game, you should have seen him taking them on and beating them." But you have to judge someone over a season. Alex was such a lovely guy, who you couldn't fail to like, so what could you say to him? I roomed with him on several occasions and he had this lovely way about him. He spoke pigeon English which improved as time went on and he knew how to put words together.

Harry Haslam wasn't going to leave Sabella out because he'd just paid £160,000 for him. A manager is bound to be biased about a player in that sense because it's his opinion that's seen him brought in. There are plenty of examples where a manager has stuck by a player a little bit longer than they should. Alex later joined me at Leeds and he was also a luxury player there. One of the plusses for me going to Leeds was that I got away from Alex, but 18 months later he followed me!

Tony Kenworthy suffered a knee injury against Preston, which ruled him out of the Liverpool game. Tony was a good, left-sided centre-back, who'd been the England Youth captain. He had a lot of ability and was a very aggressive player who loved a battle, always wanting to come out on top. I also picked up a knock at Preston and it was reported that I was a doubt, but I made a quick recovery. With the game being played on the Monday night, I went in for some treatment from physio Geoff Goodall on the Sunday. When we trained on the morning of the game, I had a little warm-up and felt fine. Andy Keeley came in to partner John Matthews in the centre of defence as Kenworthy's replacement. Andy had joined us from Spurs and wasn't a bad player. Matthews, who'd been signed from Arsenal as a centre-back, was later switched to midfield because he had a lot of ability and was a good passer.

Liverpool, apart from being double European Champions, had won their previous three games against QPR, Ipswich and Manchester City and few people thought we would cause an upset. But our Uruguayan coach Danny Bergara was convinced that we could win. He gave certain people roles to perform. My role was to man-mark Terry McDermott because as a fit 18 year-old, I could run up and down all day. It didn't matter who I was playing, they could never out-run me. When Liverpool got the ball, my job was to stay with McDermott. Sabella wasn't given a role at all, which bears out what I said earlier. He was like the floater in midfield, which worried me a little bit, but they had a player in the centre of midfield who wasn't particularly fit, Ray Kennedy. Their midfield was made up of Kennedy, McDermott, Graeme Souness and Steve Heighway. Out of those four, the one who was buzzing around like a fly was McDermott. I understood why I was given that role because I was playing on the left and he was on the right. I've always been taught as a footballer that if you win your individual battles, you'll probably win the game, so it was my job to try and nullify him. I had to make sure he didn't score and that's all I focused on during the game. I thought to myself that there was no way we were going to beat them, but if McDermott doesn't score, at least I've done my job. That was my personal aim. McDermott scored loads of goals, often from 25 or 30 yards out. Later, when I went to Leeds, I man-marked the likes of Liam Brady and Sammy McIlroy and it was something I never minded doing because I had reputation for being very fit.

Mick Speight marked Souness, with Stainrod going out towards the right to help John Cutbush, who was at right-back, deal with Heighway. Speight was strong, but he could play a bit as well. He would get-it-

and-give-it, making forceful runs. Stainrod played mainly in midfield at that time before playing up front later. Cutbush was a good player who came from Fulham with a good pedigree. He was a good athlete with a good attitude.

We had Steve Finnieston up front who was a good, honest centre-forward. Unfortunately, he was blighted by injuries after joining United from Chelsea.

Of the other players, Colin Franks was as hard as nails, while Paul Garner was a very accomplished left-back, who was a fantastic tackler with a good engine. He was also one of the nicest lads I've ever met.

When the game got underway, I set up Alan Woodward for possibly the best chance of the first-half. I crossed the ball to the near post and Woody got to it just before the defender, but he put his effort wide. Also in the first-half, there was a great incident when the referee, Derek Lloyd, booked the whole of the Liverpool wall – McDermott, Kenny Dalglish, Jimmy Case and Phil Neal – for not retreating far enough.

Dalglish hit the inside of the post in the second-half, with the ball rolling right across the line and staying out. Cutbush also cleared off the line from Souness as Liverpool pushed men forward.

Ray Kennedy used to ghost in for headers, but that didn't happen on the night because he didn't get any opportunities. But Conroy was forced to save a ferocious Kennedy shot with his legs. Conroy was the man of the match for me. I've got to say that Steve is the most gifted goalkeeper I've ever seen and I think he should have done more in his career because he had the ability to be an outstanding goalkeeper for a long time. But he liked his golf, liked a pint and was a little bit over-weight, so people questioned his attitude. On that particular night, however, he was unbeatable.

It was still goalless with just ten minutes to go when I scored what proved to be the winner. The ball was bobbling around and Colin Franks eventually won it and nudged it to Sabella. As soon as Alex received it, I shouted, "Give it me" because I was pretty much free on the edge of the box. But he only passed it when Ray Kennedy was really close to me and I thought to myself, "What am I going to do here?" because Kennedy was just behind me, about to kick me. I just had one touch, moving the ball to my left, before popping it with my left foot. It was a very hard shot with a bit of curl and it was probably one of the sweetest shots I ever struck. I didn't have any run up to it, it was just a case of pulling the trigger, hitting it and thankfully it went into the corner of the net.

When I first hit it, I thought it was going wide, but because I'd put some swerve on the ball – 'tuzzy' as I call it – it went in. It must have been just millimetres from hitting the post. Ray Clemence dived hard to try and keep it out, but he was never going to get it. It must have been a ball width between his fingers tips and the post.

It was like a dream come true. As soon as it went in, I turned and ran towards the John Street Stand, looking for my family. As well as my mum and dad, there was my wife, who was my girlfriend at the time, and other family members. All the players piled on top of me as we celebrated.

I can't remember anything about the last ten minutes, to be honest, because I was on such a high. But I know that they threw men forward and we had to defend for our lives. I'd obviously done my job well against McDermott because at one stage he turned to me and said, "I wish you'd just f*** off!" The Liverpool players didn't take the defeat well. I can remember Souness saying we were lucky and refusing to sign autographs for fans after walking off the pitch.

Either side of the game against us, Liverpool thrashed Manchester City 4-1 at Maine Road and then thrashed Spurs 7-0. They went on to win the League Championship by eight points, losing just four games in the process. Given they were also European Cup holders, it was really a result you could never have predicted. It was probably one of the biggest upsets of the century, in my opinion, because they were a helluva team and they didn't put out a weakened side.

Haslam told people afterwards that we never did anything different for the Liverpool game, but his assistant Danny Bergara was apparently seen in cafeterias, using salt pots to show anyone who'd listen how he went about his master plan. I'm sure it was all down to Danny because he was a good tactician. He used to do things in training which were strange at the time, like check your pulse and your recovery time. That sort of approach was quite rare in '78, so it's fair to say he was ahead of his time.

The whole club was on a high after the game, but we soon got brought back down to earth because we lost 2-0 at home to Crystal Palace the following Saturday and lost 4-1 at home to Leeds in the next round of the League Cup.

I was looking forward to the Leeds game, but it was like an anti-climax. They were ready for us and killed us off very quickly. Former United legend Tony Currie was outstanding and Eddie Gray played well. I thought on the night I played really well.

I think there were one or two players in the team who'd made their mind up that they wanted to leave United. Some of them thought they were better than what they were. They felt they didn't have to go out and work to get the result, they thought it would just come. That's a very dangerous thing because you've got no divine right to win a game. When you go onto a football pitch, you have to work your socks off to make sure you win and that wasn't happening. People were passing the buck and thinking, "Someone will score a goal, I'll just do my bit." No-one wanted to do that little bit extra to win a game. Being a young lad, I just wanted to work my socks off and do my best in every game. But there were players in that team who just wouldn't work as hard as they should have done. We never really thought we were going to get relegated. It was only in the last two or three games that we realised we were in danger. My dad watched all the games and I remember saying to him, "If we're not careful, we're going to get relegated." We ended up going down to Division Three after winning only once in our last seven games, finishing just a point behind Charlton.

If the fans from that era had to pick a team with all their favourites in, Alex Sabella would be in it. But I think that if we hadn't signed him, we wouldn't have got relegated. I've got no axe to grind, I'm just saying it how it is. Football's a team game and you want all 11 players pulling in the same direction. He wouldn't have got into my team, unless he changed the way he played. He should have worked a bit harder and waited to do his magic in the final third instead of around the half-way line. I would have tried to change him slightly by working with him on the training pitch, encouraging him to close people down and release the ball a little bit sooner. That's the way I would have coached his faults out of him, but Bergara wasn't going to do that because he was a Uruguayan who was brought up to play that way.

I didn't make my feelings public about Sabella back then. I only told my family what I thought. My dad felt the same way about Sabella. "He never gives you the ball," he'd often say after a game. It's only now, nearly twenty years later, that I'm saying he wasn't the right player at that time for the club.

Despite the fact that we were relegated, I was playing well and I knew that Leeds, QPR and other clubs had been watching me. Dave Bentley, the Leeds chief scout, watched me in the Liverpool game and I think they kept tabs on me from then until the end of the season. The season before, I also had a really good game against Sunderland at Bramall Lane. Jimmy Adamson was the manager of Sunderland then, before taking over at Leeds, and I think he had an eye on me for a period of time.

Lots of fans came up to me at the end of the season and told me they didn't want me to leave. I assured them I wouldn't because I was fully committed to United, but Haslam agreed to sell me to Leeds for £140,000. The fact that I had a six-year contract meant the power was with the club. It's not like it is nowadays, with freedom of contract.

Haslam likened me to Eric Gates at Ipswich. "You're very similar, but he scores more goals than you," he said. He tried to make it look as if they were selling me for tactical reasons, but there was no way that was the case. It was made easier because Sabella and I played in the same position and we were both good players. I don't want to sound big-headed, but I was a good player. Haslam probably thought he would get rid of me and give Alex a free rein on the left. Mick Speight and Simon Stainrod were still there as well. Haslam was a wily old character who'd been around the block a few times. 'Happy Harry', as he was known, knew what to say at the right time. I haven't got a high opinion of him as a person, for reasons I'll keep to myself. Professionally speaking, I shouldn't have been allowed to leave and the same goes for the likes of Simon Stainrod, Keith Edwards and Ian Benjamin. None of us wanted to leave.

I was picked up by Dave Bentley and taken up to Elland Road. I was on my own, at the age of 19, without anyone to guide me and it was an intimidating experience. I didn't get involved in contract negotiations because Jimmy Adamson told me what they were going to pay me. I was given plenty of advice beforehand, but when you're sitting in a room with Adamson, who was a tough-talking Geordie, all of that goes out of the window. He said, "We want you because we think we can make you into a player." I thought to myself, "Well, I thought I was a player." I was then taken to a heart specialist and given various tests, all on the same day, even though I hadn't actually said I'd sign for them. I was overawed by the whole experience and just signed what was put in front of me. I could have signed on a piece of toilet paper for all I cared because I felt intimated. I signed because I thought that was what was expected of me at a big club like Leeds. I didn't have the balls to say that I wanted to speak to my wife, my mum and dad and Harry Haslam before making a decision over the following week. That's what I should have done. You got five per cent of the fee over the period of your contract as a signing on fee, which turned out to be peanuts.

As I've said, I never wanted to leave United, to be honest. The fans were great to me and I loved the club and wanted to help get them back up. I'd also just got married and had a son, but I felt rail-roaded into leaving. By the time I was transferred to Leeds, I'd played over a hundred games, which was a record total of appearances for a teenager at United.

We should never have got relegated in the 1978/79 season. But they under-achieved again two seasons later and went down to the Fourth Division. When they were beating teams easily in Division Four, they were in a false position because they should never have been there in the first place. It was a mis-match because they should never have been playing the likes of Lincoln and Aldershot. I remember observing it when I was at Leeds because I always looked out for United's results. The club should always be in the top two divisions because that's where they deserve to be.

During my time at Leeds, I suffered a serious knee injury at the age of 22 and went three years without kicking a ball. When I did come back, I wasn't the same player. Operations back then were not the same as they are now. I popped both cartilages at the same time, but because the surgeon didn't spot it during the first operation, I couldn't get fit. The operation was done on the NHS because the club surgeon had damaged his finger in a gardening accident. So instead of having the expertise of a top-class surgeon, I had an NHS surgeon who took out my cartilage. I found out a year later that I'd actually popped both cartilages, but he didn't spot the other one. They eventually injected ink into my knee and discovered that my cartilage was torn and they were 99 per cent certain it was torn during the original injury.

I was released by Leeds in the summer of 1986 and joined Bristol City, but I was there only five months before moving to Port Vale. I was forced to quit playing due to injury at the age of 29. It was officially my right ankle, but my knee was close to going anyway, so it was really a combination of the two problems. I was told that I could have probably carried on playing for another two years, but I risked ending up in a wheelchair in later years. But now at the age of 46, because I packed in when I did, I'm coaching and going on running machines. The surgeon who operated on me when I was 21 was spot on. "I'll get you playing again, but you'll pack in at 29," he told me. He also said, "You might need an artificial knee at fiftyish." I hope he's wrong on that one because I've only got four years to go.

I had a season as Port Vale's reserve team/youth team coach, along with Mike Pejic and enjoyed it. I was put on a terrible wage and told it would be increased after a year. But at the end of the season, Port Vale were promoted and the chairman Bill Bell said, "I know I said I'd give you a rise, but there's no money in the pot because we need it for players." So I jacked it in and took my company car back on the Sunday. Bell tried to get me to change my mind and offered me more money, but I didn't want to know. I said, "You would have got me for the least amount possible, but now you're saying there's money in the pot to give me…"

I was angry and disillusioned with the people who run football clubs, so I decided to walk away from the professional game altogether and went to work for a company called Refuge Assurance. It was just supposed to be a stop-gap because I planned to study to become a physiotherapist. After all the injuries I've had, I thought I'd be ideal for that. But I took to the financial industry like a duck to water. I got the equivalent of a degree in financial services and now I run my own company with a business partner. We employ around twenty staff and we've got four offices after buying an IFA practice in Leicester. Over the next ten years I want to make a good living.

I'm still involved in football on an administrative basis as an agent and on a voluntary basis as a coach and I still love it. I represent Celtic's Aidan McGeady, who's the son of ex-United winger John 'Speedy' McGeady. I'm a good coach with the kids I work with and they've won the league we compete in for three years running. I coached at non-league level as well and had a fair degree of success, but I don't do it now because my business interests have grown over the last three years. It's got to a level now where I can only coach the under-15s. I also cover matches for the Press Association, mainly in the East Midlands.

I've got to be honest and say that football is a very insular industry and, once you're outside of it, some people don't want to know you. If you walked into a room and there were thirty people in there, twenty of them being footballers and the rest non-footballers, in a short period of time those twenty would gravitate to one side of the room, leaving the other ten. That's why I don't want to get back into professional football. I'm not really bothered because my main priorities are my family and my business, but it would be nice if someone would take a bit of time out to chat about old times.

I've spent most of my adult life in Yorkshire and the people are down to earth. Although I spent seven years at Leeds, Sheffield United are my favourite club because I spent my happiest time there. I still keep a close eye on what's happening at United. I met my wife in Sheffield, so I've got great memories of the city as well.

I had 13 or 14 years in the First and Second Divisions, but it's just a shame that I had the injury problems which cut my career short. Scoring against Liverpool turned out to be the most memorable moment of my career. I later played in big Cup games and in European ties for Leeds, but the Liverpool game was the biggest one I played in. I remember the game as if it were yesterday and have a lasting reminder of that goal in the shape of a watercolour painting, which hangs proudly on a wall at my home.

TONY KENWORTHY
DEFENDER 1976–1986

BORN   30 October 1958, Leeds
SIGNED   July 1976 from Apprentice
BLADES CAREER   324 games, 36 goals
HONOURS   Fourth Division Championship 1981/82, promotion from Division Three 1983/84
LEFT   Transferred to Mansfield, March 1986

A tough-tackling defender whose no-nonsense style endeared him to Blades supporters. Tony played either at left-back or in central defence and was an assured penalty-taker. After being tipped for a bright future as a youngster, he was unlucky to play most of his football in the lower divisions, with injury problems hampering his career.

Sheffield United 1 v Arsenal 0

League Cup Second Round first leg
Tuesday 7 October 1981

Bramall Lane
Attendance 19,101

Fourth Division United shoot down the First Division Gunners in the League Cup

Teams

Ian Porterfield	**Managers**	Terry Neill
Keith Waugh	1	Pat Jennings
John Ryan	2	John Devine
Stewart Houston	3	Kenny Sansom
Paul Richardson	4	Brian Talbot
John McAlle	5	David O'Leary
Tony Kenworthy	6	Willie Young
Steve Neville	7	John Hollins
Mike Trusson	8	Alan Sunderland
Paul Garner	9	John Hawley
Bob Hatton	10	Peter Nicholas
Steve Charles	11	Paul Davis
Hatton 59	**Scorers**	

Referee: J Hunting

As A KID growing up in Leeds, I played for Leeds City Boys and Yorkshire Boys. I could have gone to Liverpool, Leeds or West Brom, but I went to Sheffield United basically because John Short, who was the youth coach at Bramall Lane, badgered my parents. I used to go to Liverpool and Leeds in my school holidays, but I felt at home at Sheffield United, so I felt an affiliation with the club from an early age.

I was a midfield player when I was at school. But one day when I was playing in a Leeds City Schools game, they needed someone to step in and I was asked to play at the back. I just stuck in defence from then on and went to United as a defender.

When I first joined United, just a few days after leaving school, the majority of apprentices were Sheffield lads. Ken Furphy was the manager and I don't really think he fancied me as a young player at the time. Furphy got the sack and fortunately for me, Jimmy Sirrell came in as Furphy's replacement and took a shine to me. He also liked Simon Stainrod and we both broke into the first-team towards the end of the 1975/76 season when United were in the old First Division. Keith Edwards came in a bit later and we ended up being in digs together. I was captain of the England Youth team at the time, playing with players like Kenny Sansom, Gordon Cowans, Sammy Lee, Simon Stainrod and Chris Turner.

I made my debut at Norwich in April 1976 as the club struggled to stay in the First Division. A week before that I had been an unused substitute in the game at Tottenham. Stainrod made his debut against Spurs as we lost 5-0. The following week, I got a call to go to the Ball Inn training ground to play in a triallists game with some young kids who were coming through. I thought to myself, "I'm taking a backwards step here." I don't know if Sirrell was testing me out, but just a few days later I made my debut at Norwich. I played alongside Eddie Colquhoun in central defence and we won 3-1.

I had also been a substitute a few weeks before at Manchester City after a player went down ill. I was due to play for the youth team when I got a call to go to Maine Road. I actually got fined because I should have been in my digs. I used to go home to Leeds on Friday night and my father would bring me back on the Saturday to play in the youth team. People from the club were chasing me all over the place and when they finally made contact with me, I got a right bollocking from Jimmy Sirrell for a start and got fined a week's wages for not being where I should have been. I ended up sitting on the bench and never got on. We got beat 4-0.

After receiving the call to go over to Maine Road, it was strange to be in the dressing room with players like Tony Currie, Alan Woodward and Jim Brown – players I'd only really seen on TV. I'd cleaned their boots, but not been near them much because apprentices never really spoke to first-team players at that time, so I was a bit star-struck.

There was no big fuss made when I was named in the side for the Norwich match. I just went in the dressing room after training and saw my name on the team-sheet. It was a case of getting my suit and everything because I was on my way with the team to Norwich on Friday. As a young lad, I found it very un-nerving to be on the coach with no-one speaking to me and the rest of the players all doing their own thing.

That first night away with the team, I was rooming with Colquhoun and he didn't say two words to me. I was sat in bed watching TV while he read a book. When it was about half past nine, he just closed the book and turned the light off, which was my cue to go to sleep! When we got to the ground, the players' football-mode clicked in and they would give you bits of advice. But they stuck to doing their own thing again on the way home. Gradually, you work your way in to that kind of situation and they just accept you.

It was fantastic to be able to play in a team that fielded Tony Currie. He deserves to be labelled a legend because he was a world-class player who would be worth millions today. It was a pleasure to play alongside him. Jim Brown was a quality goalkeeper who was a Scotland international. Colquhoun had also been capped by Scotland and playing alongside him only improved me as a player.

Paul Garner came in from Huddersfield with a decent reputation. He was a very under-rated defender who was quick and fit. We played together later at Mansfield, so we more or less followed each other around. Mick Speight was a solid midfield player who was Sheffield United through and through. He hated to lose and it was an honour to play alongside him. Gary Hamson was a good young midfielder, who went on to have a good career. He had a good touch and a good engine, getting up and down well.

I am indebted to Jimmy Sirrell because he gave me my chance. He was quite an eccentric man, but he gave me a lot of encouragement. He was a great coach and a complete and utter football man. But the club was on a downward spiral at that time and it went a bit pear-shaped for him. We were relegated at the end of the 1975/76 season after finishing at the bottom of Division One and finished a disappointing 11th the following term. When Sirrell left early in the 1977/78 season, a lot of players were getting old and it was going to be a complete and utter rebuilding job for whoever came in. Players like Woodward and Colquhoun had been round the block a couple of times and age was catching up with them. The club had also got into debt after building the New South Stand. I still remember around that time, the early Eighties, people were taking light bulbs out to save money because United were struggling.

Cec Coldwell, who had been at the club for years as a player and coach, had a spell as caretaker-manager following Sirrell's departure. They didn't have the man they wanted in place at the time, so they gave him a chance and I think he did well. We went on a good little run, but then had a bad run and the alarm bells started ringing, so Harry Haslam was brought in from Luton. Haslam's style of management was completely different. Danny Bergara was his first-team coach and Danny more or less did it all. You wouldn't see Harry from Monday to Friday because all the coaching was left to Danny, who was an exceptional coach as he proved in his later career as manager of Stockport County. He was young and very enthusiastic. He had been a quality footballer himself and he could still do it at that time in training, so he had the full respect of the players. Harry was a suit-manager who worked behind the scenes. He came in now and again, but never took a training session. Harry would come in an hour before kick-off. "All the best, boys. Get out and do it," he'd say to us. It worked for them to a certain extent.

Haslam was more or less the founder of bringing foreigners in. He was on a scouting trip to Argentina which resulted in Ossie Ardiles and Ricky Villa going to Tottenham. The story goes that he tried to sign Diego Maradona before bringing in another Argentinian, Alex Sabella. Haslam also signed Pedro Verde and Len de Goey. Alex would still be in his suit at ten to three, but then you'd turn round and he'd be ready to go, with his socks rolled down. Foreign players at that time had a different mentality to us, simply because they didn't like the cold. They also didn't like training on Fridays and only understood English when it suited them. When you look at Alex, he was a fantastic footballer and a great lad, but would you want to go to war with him alongside you?

When you had to go to Hillsborough or somewhere like that, you knew he was going to get the shit kicked out of him basically. But players like Alex would get you goals, so you would forgive them for the tracking back they didn't do because the hardest job of all is putting the ball in the back of the net. Our job was to make sure we didn't concede goals and give them the ball. De Goey came from Holland and was more of an English type of player, who would get stuck in. He didn't last long in English football because there was no-one there to help him. He was just left to get on with it, not like today where foreign players are given a lot of help.

We were relegated to Division Three at the end of the 1978/79 season and the further we dropped down the divisions, the more that teams came to Bramall Lane and fancied a game. The pitch was fantastic, the stadium was one of the biggest around and the support was always tremendous, so opposition players often raised their game. It was always like a Cup-tie and you have to have some strong characters in that situation.

We played Sheffield Wednesday on Boxing Day 1979 in front of over 49,000 fans. We were going well at the time and would have gone some points clear if we'd have beaten them. I remember being in the tunnel, waiting to go out, when things started kicking off. John MacPhail was fighting with a Wednesday player called John Lowey. There was a bit of tension and I was looking forward to it because I didn't mind a bit of that. We hadn't played Wednesday for a while and we were desperate to win.

Wednesday took the lead when one of their players hit a screamer which flew into the top corner. Then Jeff Bourne fired in a free-kick which hit the crossbar, the rebound went to MacPhail who volleyed it from about six yards and the ball hit keeper Bob Bolder right in the middle of the chest. MacPhail was inconsolable at half-time, crying his eyes out because of the pressure. Then they got a penalty and it was just one of those games where everything went for them. Jeff King, who later joined United, did a great job on Sabella, kicking him up and down. He did exactly what they expected him to do. He went out to stop Alex playing and he stopped him in every way. We just couldn't get our game going and I think the defeat wrecked our season.

We went up to play Dundee in the Anglo-Scottish Cup that season and beat them, with MacPhail scoring the goal. It was John's old team and he was outstanding that day. Jock Stein, who was the Scotland manager at the time, came to watch John play against St Mirren later in the competition and we got beat. If he'd have watched him play against Dundee, he would have played for Scotland, but he watched him in the St Mirren game when we lost and that's how football goes. Steve Conroy, who broke his arm against St Mirren, was a good keeper. Les Tibbott would be the first name on your team-sheet because he'd give you everything he'd got. Steve Finnieston scored goals for Chelsea and was always difficult to play against, but he was quite injury-prone. John Matthews was a class player who was a great passer of the ball with good vision, but he would also put his foot in, which is what you need. There were players coming in and going out, so there was no continuity in the team and Haslam wasn't a young man. He'd done so well at Luton, but he was at a big club and things weren't going too well.

Martin Peters was brought in as player/coach and he took over when Haslam stood down. We didn't get on and I had no time for him. Don't get me wrong, I respected him as a footballer after what he had achieved in the game. That was without question. But he was aloof as a person and, as a motivator and man-manager, he wasn't for me. Peters didn't like my style of football. He wanted to play a bit of football and didn't like players putting a foot in. I liked to get involved, but he didn't like that and we had argument after argument after games when I'd kicked somebody a bit harder than he liked. But that was my game because I wanted to win at all costs. Sometimes I'd see him pull out of tackles and I didn't like that. I'm not disrespecting him, I think that was just the way he played.

I could have gone to Leeds or Everton. There was also talk of Nottingham Forest being interested. The season after, Forest won the European Cup. Then Mike Watterson, who had taken over as chairman of Derby County, approached me. It was bizarre because Watterson phoned me at home one afternoon and basically said, "Within two or three hours, you'll be a Derby County player." He never asked me if I wanted to go!

At around nine o'clock that evening, Watterson phoned back. "Look, we can't agree a fee," he told me. He still didn't ask me whether I wanted to go or not and that was the last I heard from him.

You get to April time and all of a sudden you think to yourself, "Hang on a minute, this is not going well for us." I didn't like the atmosphere in the dressing room at that time. "I'll still be here at the end of the season and you players will be gone," Peters would say. Players get jittery and they don't need to hear things like that. Cec Coldwell was still on the coaching staff, but Peters took most of the training at that time.

Peter Anderson, who had been on loan at United, took over as manager of Millwall and he wanted to sign myself and John MacPhail as a partnership.

But again the club squashed it. I got a call from Harry Haslam, who was still living near Worksop after leaving United, asking me to go over and see him. When I went over to his house, he got David Pleat on the phone. Pleat was in charge of Luton and he wanted to sign me. I was really happy at United, but I was tempted to leave because of my relationship with Peters and there were also these people whispering in my ear, so I was talking to clubs, which was of course against the rules.

We faced Walsall on the last day of the season and they needed to win to stay up and send us down. I was getting changed when Peters came in and told me I wasn't playing, so I put my gear back on. That was the way he was treating me at the time. We looked set to achieve safety when we were awarded a penalty late in the game. I would have taken the penalty if I'd been playing. In my absence, John Matthews was supposed to take it, but he didn't fancy it, so Don Givens took it. I'm not being disrespectful to Don, but he didn't have that affiliation with the club. He was a journeyman who was coming to the end of his career and did it mean that much to him? He mishit the penalty and the keeper saved it. Walsall scored the penalty they were awarded just afterwards and we were relegated.

Peters tried to sell me to his old club Norwich who were in the First Division at the time. A team-mate called John Ryan – who had played with Peters at Norwich – tried to persuade me to go when we chatted in a bar during our end of season trip to Spain. "Look, you should go because it would be a good career move for you," he said. "He doesn't like you and he's going to try and off-load you at every opportunity." But the more they tried to get me to go, the more I dug my heels in. Although I wanted to play at a higher standard of football, I desperately wanted to do that with Sheffield United. Funnily enough, Peters quit when we were in Spain, so I got a reprieve.

After dropping down to the Fourth Division, you can only go one way from there. Reg Brealey came in as the new chairman and it was one of the best things that happened to the club at the time. He had some money to put in and he brought in Ian Porterfield as manager. Porterfield, who had just taken Rotherham up, was young and enthusiastic. It was a great appointment. He had a completely different attitude to what we'd had the season before and I got on really well with him. His motivational skills were fantastic and he made you feel brilliant. He completely lifted the club and there was a good buzz around the place.

We enjoyed a good start to the season and were drawn to face Arsenal in the second round of the League Cup after beating York in the opening round. They were two-legged ties in those days and we were at home in the first leg. We were going into the game as the underdogs and had nothing to lose because our main aim was to win promotion. We were flying at the time and confidence was high.

Porterfield was more thorough than the managers we'd had before. He gave us reports on each player, so you knew your opponents. He was a young manager wanting to do well. Motivation was a big thing with him and he made you feel good, so you wanted to go out and play for him.

Porterfield had switched me to left-back and given me a free rein to do what I wanted, which meant I got forward a bit more and took free-kicks. But I reverted to central defence for the Arsenal game due to an injury to John MacPhail. At 5ft 11ins tall, I wasn't big for a central defender, but it was a position I enjoyed because I was a decent athlete and enjoyed getting involved. I played with the likes of Eddie Colquhoun, MacPhail and Paul Stancliffe during my career, who were all bigger than me. MacPhail was a quality defender and I enjoyed playing alongside him. We'd split the pitch down the left and right, so he wouldn't come and dominate in the air if I felt I could go and win the ball.

I played alongside John McAlle against Arsenal with Stewart Houston taking my normal place at left-back. John Ryan, who played at right-back, completed our defence and we had Keith Waugh in goal. Defender Paul Garner was pushed into midfield alongside Paul Richardson, Mike Trusson and Steve Charles. We were without our prolific goalscorer Keith Edwards, who was cup-tied after playing for Hull earlier in the competition, so Steve Neville partnered Bob Hatton in attack.

Arsenal had international quartet Pat Jennings, David O'Leary, Kenny Sansom and Peter Nicholas in their side, as well as experienced top-flight players like Brian Talbot, Willie Young, John Hollins and Alan Sunderland. They were without injured England midfielder Graham Rix on the left hand side of their midfield, but it was otherwise pretty much a full-strength Gunners line-up.

We competed effectively from the start with Charles unlucky to see his fiercely struck shot go narrowly wide early on. Trusson also threatened to give us a first-half lead when he fired in a firm drive after chesting the ball down, but Sansom got a challenge in to take the sting out of the shot. We went into the half-time interval at 0-0. Charles and Richardson had kept Talbot and Nicholas quiet in midfield and my partnership with McAlle at the back was proving to be effective, so we were pleased with the way things were going.

After being largely subdued, Arsenal looked certain to take the lead in the 58th minute when they launched a rare attack. Paul Davis was sent clear and found himself one-on-one with Waugh, but Keith did superbly well to claim the ball at his feet. From there, Waugh launched the ball forward with a strong kick and an Arsenal defender only succeeded in heading the ball into the path of Bob Hatton, who controlled before firing low past Jennings in front of an ecstatic Kop. Hatton was a handful because he was a big, strong man.

We threatened to go further ahead, but Jennings pulled off a good save to keep out an effort from Neville. Arsenal threw players forward in the last ten minutes in the hope of salvaging a draw to take back to Highbury for the second leg. They hit the woodwork and Waugh, who had a great season, made a couple of brilliant saves to keep out efforts from Talbot and Hollins. We were delighted with a clean-sheet and I was pleased with my own performance. Tony Pritchett, who covered United for Sheffield newspaper *The Star* nominated me as his man of the match. "Faultless in defence" was how he described my performance.

When you look at that Arsenal line-up, it was a quality team. It's only when you look back after you've finished that you realise what a good achievement it was to beat a team like that. At the time, you just get on with the next game. We had a decent side and I think it would be a decent Championship team now.

Porterfield praised his chief scout, John McSeveney, for providing a detailed analysis of how Arsenal played. John and Jim Dixon had followed Porterfield from Rotherham and they were a good team. Arsenal manager Terry Neill acknowledged that we had played well, but he pointed out that it was only the first leg.

We travelled to Highbury for the second leg on the back of a good 2-0 away win over promotion rivals Bradford. Porterfield made just one change to the side from the first leg with Trenton Wiggan replacing Paul Garner in midfield. Defender Willie Young gave Arsenal a first-half lead to level the tie on aggregate, but we managed to hold on to force extra-time. Alan Sunderland scored early in extra-time and that proved to be the winner, so we had given a good account of ourselves.

It would have been nice to have made further progress in the League Cup, but promotion was our priority and we went on to win the title. There were some good teams in the division, but I think we had just a bit more quality than them. Bringing a quality goalscorer like Keith Edwards back to play in a decent side, against the opposition we were playing, meant he was always going to score goals. When the ball dropped to him in the box, nine times out of ten he would hit the target and he was quick as well. People would sometimes question his work-rate, but I watch a lot of football now and I've never seen a better finisher than Keith. Bob Hatton, who was a very good footballer, did a lot of spade work for Edwards. Colin Morris was difficult to mark on the wing and Mike Trusson was a good midfield player who scored a lot of goals.

The potential of the club is massive and the support we received just echoed that. They tried unsuccessfully to switch the last game of the season, away at Darlington, to Middlesbrough's Ayresome Park ground because of the level of support. There was a crowd of over 12,000 and I remember fans sat round edge of the pitch. We won 2-0 to clinch the championship and in the first season of three points for a win we finished with 96.

I scored 16 goals that season. I took free-kicks from around the box and got up for corners, as well as being the regular penalty-taker. With Porterfield's attention to detail, I'd get a report telling me which way the keeper went if he'd faced a penalty the week before.

I started having injury problems in the early eighties and had two ankle ligament operations which kept me out for most of the following season. At one stage, the surgeon who operated on me said, "Buy a pub because you're never going to play again." But I worked hard to get back and managed to do that, but the ankle went again on the other side, keeping me out for another spell. I played against Leeds and suffered a dislocated knee following a challenge from my old team-mate Gary Hamson. I lost about three seasons in total due to injury.

I went on loan to Mansfield before signing permanently and had unbelievable success there under Ian Greaves. We won promotion and lifted the Freight Rover Cup, beating Bristol City at Wembley. My old United team-mates John MacPhail, Steve Neville and Keith Waugh were in the Bristol side. It went to penalties and I scored the winning one. It was a great way to end my career, winning at Wembley.

It was a completely different outlook on the game at Mansfield. United are a massive club and everything was done properly there, but at Mansfield you had to grab pieces of kit where you could. We also had to train wherever we could. But there was great spirit there and we had some good players like George Foster, Neil Whatmore and Keith Cassells.

I suffered a broken jaw, broken cheekbone, broken nose and fractured eye socket playing in a game against Nottingham Forest. It was a freak elbowing incident and took me about six months to get back. Then I snapped my Achilles tendon and that was basically it. I was only 30. I went to New Zealand for a season and enjoyed it there.

I worked for the Scottish Football Association after coming back from New Zealand, doing a bit of coaching with kids. Then I got a call from Reg Brealey who invited me to work for him at Darlington. Reg had taken over the club and he wanted me to work as a consultant. I also did some coaching on the youth side. I was there for about four years in some capacity or other.

When Reg took Grantham Town on, I became manager. Danny Bergara had been the manager and when things weren't going too well, I received a phone call asking me to take over. They were full-time in the Dr Martens Premier League. We had a season there together, but I think that was enough for Reg and he pulled out in 1999. It wasn't easy and we were glad to get out of there. I had chances to go to other non-league clubs, but I'd had enough of the non-league scene. Reg still hankers after being involved in football, even though he's in his seventies now. He was good to me and I still see him every now and again. I visit his hotel in Lincolnshire and leave without paying the bill, which is nice!

I'm now living in the north-east. I've got a young family – a boy of four and a girl of six – so they take most of my time up. I cover games for the Press Association, providing statistics. I also work for Premier League Productions as a floor manager at Newcastle United. I look after the foreign journalists who are reporting on games at St James's Park, helping them to get whoever they want to interview. It's nice to be involved with the game. I love football and the game has been good to me. I'm just a lad off a council estate who could kick a ball just a little bit better than somebody else and that gave me a fantastic lifestyle.

I loved the time I was at Sheffield United. I feel as though I could just walk in there and hang my gear up, like I did years ago. After I left to join Mansfield, it took me a long time to disassociate myself from the club. I felt that the shirt was mine and that the place where I changed in the dressing room was mine. It took me a long time to come to terms with that. In fact, I do still miss the club because it means that much to me. On the occasions when I have visited there, the memories come flooding back.

I think Neil Warnock has done a great job at United. Full credit to him and his players because they've done fantastically well to get up to the Premiership. That's where they should be because it is a Premiership club.

KEITH EDWARDS
FORWARD 1975–1978/1981–1986

BORN   16 July 1957, Stockton-on-Tees
SIGNED   1 – August 1975 from Apprentice
2 – September 1981 from Hull City, £100,000
BLADES CAREER   (two spells) 297 games, 163 goals
HONOURS   Division Four Championship 1981/82, Promotion from Division Three 1983/84
LEFT   1 – Transferred to Hull City, August 1978; £60,000
2 – Transferred to Leeds United, August 1986; £125,000

A clinical finisher whose prolific goalscoring record assured him of legendary status at Bramall Lane. After being off-loaded to Hull early in his career, he returned to the club and played a key role in United's rise from Division Four. The two Golden Boots he won for his goalscoring exploits along the way are on display in United's Hall of Fame. Keith is still a regular visitor to the Lane in his role as a match summariser for BBC Radio Sheffield.

Sheffield United 4 v Gillingham 0

League Division Three
Saturday 27 August 1983

Bramall Lane
Attendance 10,405

*Edwards blasts four goals on opening day of the season
as United get off to a flying start*

Teams

Ian Porterfield	**Managers**	Keith Peacock
Keith Waugh	1	Ron Hillyard
Bob Atkins	2	Mel Sage
Paul Garner	3	Colin Duncan
Kevin Arnott	4	John Sitton
Paul Stancliffe	5	Peter Shaw
Mick Henderson	6	Phil Handford
Colin Morris	7	Andy Woodhead
		(Sub.Wayne Stokes)
Mike Trusson	8	Dick Tydeman
Keith Edwards	9	John Leslie
Ray McHale	10	Dave Mehmet
Gary Brazil	11	Mark Weatherly

Edwards 37, 57, 77, 81	**Scorers**	

Referee: V Callow

I WORKED IN A cheese factory as a trainee salesman for two years after leaving school, but I always wanted to be a footballer. I was given a three-month trial at Sheffield United, which was very exciting. I didn't do that well on trial, but I managed to catch the eye of Alan Hodgkinson, who gave me my first break when Ken Furphy was manager. Alan, who was in charge of the reserves, felt that I deserved a contract. Surprisingly enough, I only scored one goal in the reserves during that three-month spell. It was away at Coventry when David Bradford set me up and we won 1-0. It was a special day for me because my father, who lived in London, had come up to watch the game.

Life is full of coincidences. I had trials with Leeds, so it was nice when they ended up having to pay a lot of money for me! I was also on trial at Wolves and it was great when I scored my first goal in professional football against them. I could have signed for Leyton Orient and with my dad living in London, I was fairly keen to do that. But my dad advised me against it. I think he thought I would be better off staying in the north and I took his advice, so I took my chances with United rather than joining Leyton Orient. My employers kept my job open and if I hadn't made it as a footballer, I'd have probably gone straight back to my job and become a qualified salesman. I thoroughly enjoyed the job and the guy I worked with ended up being my best man. I think that being a late starter and working for a living helped me to adapt to professional football.

When I first joined United, I was in digs with Tony Kenworthy, Simon Stainrod and John McGeady who all got their first-team chance before me. I remember when we were all fairly established in the team, those three got £60-a-week and I got £55, which really pissed me off for a long time! I could never understand why there was a difference of £5.

It was nice to get into the team when I made my debut in the Cup at Leicester in January 1976. I had one effort kicked off the line, but I didn't have a sparkling game. We lost 3-0 and I was taken off after 64 minutes and replaced by Jimmy Johnstone. I made a handful of appearances that season as we went down to Division Two. Tony Currie was in that side and people forget that I played with him. Alan Woodward was another who was lovely to play with and a great character. There were also players like Len Badger and Billy Dearden. I loved that team and in my opinion that's still the best United side I played in.

The following season, I relaxed a little bit more and went on a goal-run, scoring in eight consecutive matches. That was a league record which stood until it was beaten by Jermain Defoe when he went on loan to Bournemouth and increased it to ten. I ended the season with 18 goals from 35 appearances, even though the team was struggling a little and I was in and out of the side.

It took me quite a while to settle down and feel comfortable. I hadn't been coached, so I wasn't the complete forward that everybody wanted me to be. If they created goalscoring chances, I was confident of knocking them in, but it was the other side of my game I needed to work on. It was the club's responsibility to help me along, but if I'm being honest, I don't think we had the people at the club at the time who were capable of doing that. I always used to keep in touch with my father, who played the biggest part in my football career, without a shadow of a doubt. The advice he gave and his help in coaching me was as good as anybody. My dad played a bit of football in the south and he was a friend of Eddie Baily, who played for Tottenham and England, but he didn't make it as a professional. He could easily have been a professional coach, though, if he'd had that opportunity.

Jimmy Sirrell and the man who replaced him, Harry Haslam, were very different personalities. I had my problems with Jimmy because, when I came into the game, I expected to be helped and coached. But all we did was play practice matches all the time and it got a bit boring. Whoever did really well in training would play. It wasn't really good enough from both angles I suppose, because maybe I wasn't doing enough in training to warrant a game on a regular basis. I expected to have more fun and to be helped with developing skills. Overall though, Jimmy was a good man because when I struggled a little bit as a young man, he defended me and I will always remember that.

When Haslam came in to replace Sirrell, he brought Danny Bergara with him, who was a really good coach. I used to stay behind and do extra training with Danny because by that time I'd learned that you needed to work a little harder to improve your skills. Bergara was great at teaching various skills and I learned a lot from him. I remember Haslam telling me I was the next Malcolm MacDonald and I thought to myself, "That's great because he's a good old player." I phoned my father and told him what Haslam had said. But the next week, he wanted to sell me to Hull City.

I phoned my father again and said, "I don't think he likes Malcolm MacDonald because he wants to sell me to Hull now!" I had established myself in the side and was enjoying my football, so I couldn't get my head round that. It was very frustrating.

When Haslam told me they'd accepted an offer from Hull City, I sorted of looked at him as if to say, "Why do you want to sell me?" I was a young player who'd done quite well. I trained well, got on with all the players and loved being at Sheffield United. I didn't visualise going anywhere else and there was no thought about money. I didn't automatically think, "I'm going to make loads of money if I go across there." As it turned out, I did get paid quite a lot more at Hull than I was earning at United, but that was never an issue. Steve Finnieston was brought in from Chelsea to replace me and he didn't do anything.

My first year at Hull was very good. I scored a lot of goals and was their Player of the Year. In fact, I was the top goalscorer in each of the three seasons I was there. It was good at Hull, but it was like a one-man show and I was never really that happy being there. There were two or three players in the team who could play and the rest were garbage. Unfortunately, one of them is the manager of England now! Steve McClaren was a very average player. But obviously great players don't necessarily make great coaches and vice versa.

I scored a lot of goals, got recognised and clubs like Newcastle and Middlesbrough were coming in for me, which was great. Eventually, Sheffield United came back in for me. It was a funny old situation when I played for Hull against United in the opening weeks of the 1981/82 season. United had been in touch with me prior to the game and they didn't phone me back for a couple of weeks, which was very annoying. I told United's representative that they had better sign me before Hull played against them. Because they hadn't been in touch, I punished them by scoring. I didn't like those type of games. I wasn't comfortable lining up against my old mate Tony Kenworthy, but that's how it has to be.

A deal was agreed between United and Hull and I returned to Bramall Lane in September 1981. It was easy for me to come back after three years away because my wife at the time wanted to return to Sheffield and we got a club house at Intake. We'd got two girls and had a third when we came back to Sheffield, so everything was great. The South Stand was complete and the new Executive Suite was done, so I felt that I was coming back to such a bigger club. It looked massive compared to Hull City. I settled in very quickly and that was important because we had to go straight back up. I knew some of the lads like Tony Kenworthy and Paul Garner, who were there from my first spell at the club, and soon got to know the other lads.

We played good football and I think we went close to being one of the best teams Sheffield United have ever had, although you have to take into account that we were in the lower divisions. I linked up with Bob Hatton up front. I'd seen him over the years and we got on great. He wanted to score all the goals and so did I. He'd got about seven goals and I'd only got two for Hull when I came back and I remember him saying to me, "You'll find that I'll be top goalscorer this season." I replied, "Well, I know what you mean, you've got a good start, but I don't really think that's going to happen; not when I'm back at my club." It was a good bit of banter and it didn't take me too long to catch him up.

We made goals for each other and I enjoyed playing with him. He was a great player to be alongside at that time and we complemented each other. Colin Morris then came in and took my best pal's place. Steve Neville was always my best pal and I was disappointed for him because he knew he was going to be on his way then. I just hit it off with Colin because he had great talent. We got on and had a great understanding. He's the best player I've played with. To justify that, I have to say that I played with Tony Currie, but not on a regular basis. If Colin had made you three goals, he didn't mind going back down and making you a fourth. That was special because he carried on with his job whether it was 0-0 or 6-0. Colin could cut inside or go on the outside. We scored some great goals between us. He missed out more than anybody on playing in the top-flight. He was a great player who could do anything and he could have easily played in the First Division because he was such a strong character. It was an awful shame that he broke his leg a couple of times, which made him a bit wary of going into tackles.

We thought like a Second Division team even though we were in the Fourth. The manager, Ian Porterfield, was great and chairman Reg Brealey was absolutely fabulous. I always describe him as my favourite-ever chairman. He was always approachable when we went away on tour. We absolutely slaughtered teams because nobody could touch us in that division. We only lost a few games, which were mainly down to one or two individuals playing really badly. Keith Waugh, for example, had a nightmare at Colchester, which was the only time we were on *Match of the Day*.

Coca-Cola offered £5,000 for the first player to score 35 goals that season and I found myself competing with Bury's Craig Madden for the prize. At the end of the season, when Bury went up to Hartlepool and we were at home, Madden was one off the target and I was two off it. I heard he missed a penalty and I beat him to it to win the prize, but I learned later that he was also given £5,000. I was more pleased with the fact that I won a prize of £1,000 from the Football League for scoring the most goals in the country over the whole season. It all went into the players' pool after having a vote. My old mate Tony Kenworthy said he thought it should go in the players' pool. Bob Hatton said, "No, I think Keith should have it." I was leaning more towards Bob's opinion! But seriously, I couldn't have done it without them, so it was shared out.

Winning the Fourth Division title was my first bit of success because I'd started off in the top-flight and gone all the way down to the bottom division. When I went down to a function at the Hilton Hotel in London to collect my Golden Boot, I took my father along to the presentation. Kevin Keegan got the Golden Boot in the First Division and Gordon Davies and Ronnie Moore were the winners in the other divisions. My father and I were sat on the same table as Freddie Starr and Elton John. My dad was planted right in the middle of them and I remember feeling so nervous, worrying that he was going to embarrass me. But he got on well with them and when we later played Watford, my dad came along to watch and Elton John remembered him, which was fantastic.

Terry Curran came in from Sheffield Wednesday that summer and played some great games. A lot of the fans thought we clashed, but that wasn't the case at all. He was a bit of a character and we got on very well. But it was a big ask for the fans to accept Terry because he'd done so much for Wednesday and it didn't really work out for him.

A few games into the 1982/83 season, I was relegated to the substitutes bench. I wasn't given the benefit of the doubt, in my opinion, that I'd get through a little sticky patch and go back on the goalscoring trail again. That was fairly hard to take because there wasn't anything such as squad rotation back then; the best players played and that was it. That sort of problem happened a lot with Ian Porterfield. He did it to me again the following season when I had a lengthy spell on the bench as Peter Withe and Colin Morris were preferred up front. I didn't accept it when I was told, "Well, it's horses for courses." I enlightened him that horses run round right-handed tracks, left-handed tracks, jump hurdles and run on the flat. A football pitch is a football pitch and it's the same thing week-in, week-out.

I found it difficult to accept not being in the side because I think there should have always been a place for a goalscorer who scored goals. Goals

Goalkeeper Gilmar is stranded as I score a second goal on my
England debut against Brazil at Wembley. I couldn't have asked
for a better start to my international career.

That's me (left), in training at White Hart Lane with West Brom's Ray Barlow
for England's 2-1 victory over Scotland in April 1957.

I'm pictured here (right) with Blades stalwart Alf Ringstead,
who was a fine outside-left for United in the Fifties.

I was presented with this framed newspaper report on the pitch
at half-time in a game at Bramall Lane to mark the fiftieth anniversary
of my debut for United.

What a save! I was at full stretch to keep out Chelsea in this game
at Stamford Bridge in November 1955.

Preparing for my England debut against Scotland in 1957, here I pick up
a few tips from striker Derek Kevan (left) of West Brom and legendary
captain Billy Wright (centre) of Wolves.

Billy Russell, who was the hat-trick hero in our Cup win at Newcastle, all three goals coming in a 12-minute spell.

Here I am putting Stefan Klos through his paces during my time as the goalkeeping coach at Rangers.

The 1970/71 promotion-winning squad. I'm on the back row, second from left. Others who appear in this book are Tony Currie (back row, third from right) and Alan Hodgkinson (middle row, third from right).

Manager John Harris, who handed the captaincy to me in 1965, guided us to promotion in his second spell in charge.

Behind the bar at my pub, The Fox & Goose, near Chesterfield.

I joined United as a striker, before being switched to midfield after a chat with manager John Harris and then won 17 England caps.

My form in the mid-70s attracted the attention of Manchester United boss Tommy Docherty, who wanted me to replace Bobby Charlton.

I have an office at the Academy, working as United's Football In The Community Officer.

GARY HAMSON – 1979
SHEFFIELD UNITED 1 v LIVERPOOL 0

The 1978/79 squad, featuring the players who played in the memorable League Cup win over European champions Liverpool. I'm on the front row, second from left. Tony Kenworthy is on the back row, second from left.

Programme from the Liverpool match. The biggest game of my United career.

TONY KENWORTHY – 1981
SHEFFIELD UNITED 1 v ARSENAL 0

I'm shown here with a Blades shirt I wore in the 1981/82 season. It took me a long time to get used to the fact that I was no longer a United player.

The programme from the game against Gillingham, when I scored all four goals.

I enjoy going back to the Lane, which I do on a regular basis as a match pundit on local radio.

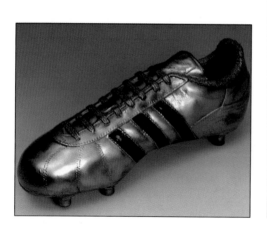

My second Golden Boot, which I won after scoring 33 league goals in the 1983/84 season. I won my first two years earlier and went on to make it a hat-trick of awards when I was at Hull.

I made a number of moves during my career, but United will always be my club.

Brian Deane scores against Leicester
to give United a 2-1 lead.

Blades fans celebrate
promotion to the top-
flight after the thrilling
win at Leicester.

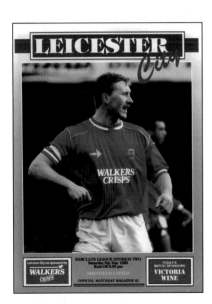

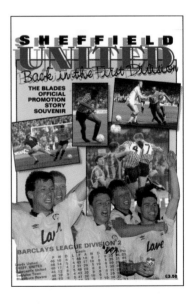

The programme from
the promotion-winning game.
I was the stand-in skipper –
what an unforgettable day!

Souvenir brochure to mark United's
return to the top-flight after 14
years. I was 32 and never thought
I'd play in the First Division.

Taking it all in as
Dave 'Harry' Bassett offers
a few instructions.

Playing for United was a dream
come true for me after supporting
the Blades as a kid.

Joy is etched on John Gannon's face as the Blades gain the upper hand in
the 1992 derby clash with Sheffield Wednesday.

Congratulated by team-mates
after another goal, this time in
the FA Cup tie against Arsenal
in January 1996.

I'm mobbed by the fans after
scoring at Highbury.

White Van Man! The vehicle I use as a self-employed courier.
The work involves early starts, but I enjoy it.

ALAN KELLY — 1998
SHEFFIELD UNITED 1 v COVENTRY CITY 1

Ticket from the FA Cup sixth round replay against Coventry.

Keeping out Simon Haworth's spot-kick to complete
a hat-trick of saves in the penalty shoot out.

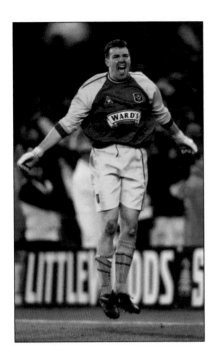

Celebrating at the end of the shoot-out. I was so pumped up, I thought the veins in my neck were going to burst!

Then I was joined by a tumult of fans, who swarmed onto the pitch.

Neil Shipperley hooks in the second goal against Hull
and we felt comfortable at 2-0.

Then, after a wobble on our part, Darryl Duffy struck Hull's equaliser.

David Unsworth celebrates his last-gasp winner,
with Chris Morgan in hot pursuit.

It's always nice to win awards and here's one I picked up in the
2005/06 season. I was also named United's Player of the Year.

Playing in the Premier League has already provided
some great occasions, such as my last-minute winner against
Middlesbrough to clinch our first win…

…what a great moment!

win matches, winning matches creates bigger crowds and bigger crowds create more finance. I scored a hat-trick after coming on as a substitute against Grimsby in the League Cup. I was the angriest man in the world on that particular day. Alan Young was substituted because he broke a nail! I have never been as angry in my life and I went on to prove a point. I worked hard, smashed goals in and made another one. I had plenty of fall-outs with managers, but I always made up with them. When Ian Porterfield was manager of Chelsea, he'd stay at the Moat House Hotel in Sheffield and I'd go and see him. To this day, if he is in the area, he'll give me a ring and we'll meet up.

Going into the opening game of the 1983/84 season against Gillingham, we were on a high after having a good pre-season. It's usually red hot on the opening day of the season and it was that day. There's a little bit more pressure when you're at home because you want to get off to a winning start. Maybe if you're away from home, you know there's every chance you're not going to get a win. I was slightly disappointed with the fans at the time because they were all chanting Tony Currie's name. There was talk of Currie coming back to the club, which was exciting for me because that would have been great. I'd loved to have seen him come back, even though he was in the late stages of his career. But, being competitive, when the fans were chanting Currie's name, I felt it was a little bit disrespectful to me and it gave me that gee-up that I probably needed.

I tried just a little bit harder and when I whacked the first goal in from a free-kick – the sort of goal Currie would have relished – that was my opportunity to put the chant to bed because I wanted them to chant for me. That sounds awfully selfish and conceited, but that's how you think as a professional footballer. I thought, "They're not singing for an old player while I'm on that field. I want them to sing for me."

I think people were surprised by the first goal because all of a sudden, they've seen me taking free-kicks. Ian Porterfield got me taking corners and I was good at dead-ball situations. We were getting a lot of success in pre-season from my corner kicks, so Porterfield stuck by the plan. It was totally justified because I think we got something like 20-odd goals from corners that season.

After taking corners, I was hungry to take free-kicks. I wanted to take everything, penalties, free-kicks and corners – that's the type of player I was. Whenever you get a job like taking free-kicks, you know you've got to knock something in early doors, so I was under quite a bit of pressure for the first one. As it happens, I whipped it into the top corner to the keeper's right and I was really delighted with that goal more than anything because I knew from then on that I'd be on the free-kicks on a regular basis. It was in the perfect spot for me, down the left-hand side to whip it across with my right foot. It was a big goal for me. The likes of Tony Kenworthy, Colin Morris and Kevin Arnott all wanted to take free-kicks and I knew that I'd edged them out with that goal. Anything down the left-hand side was mine from then on and I'd added something to my game.

After going into the break with a 1-0 lead, I scored a second on 57 minutes. Colin Morris beat a couple of players down the right-hand side and squared the ball to me. If I'm being perfectly honest, I scuffed the shot a little bit, but it was on target and it went in off the far post at the Kop end, which made it special.

When a player gets two goals, all he ever wants is a hat-trick because that gets the headlines. To complete my hat-trick, I got on the end of a through ball from Mike Trusson on the edge of the box and cut inside as the keeper came out to narrow the angle. I always went to the near post – which is something my father always used to teach me – and fired home at about head-height. It was a good build-up with plenty of people involved and it was a good goal.

My fourth goal was a far-post header, with Colin Morris again the provider. The ball came to the back post and I headed it back to where it came from, which is what you should always do. It just crept into the far corner. I think, to be fair, someone was following up and they could have knocked it in, but they left it.

What a start to the season! To score four goals in the first game of the season is different class. My father put Teletext on and saw 'Sheffield United 4-0 Gillingham' and thought, 'I hope that Keith has scored.' Then he saw that I'd scored all four goals. My dad's not with us now, but we've discussed that day many times in the family. They're really special times and you have to appreciate them because there are plenty of ups and downs in football. I got the match-ball of course, but I gave it away to my brother's son who is also called Keith Edwards. In fact, I've given away most of the mementoes from my career to charities. I've got my Golden Boot awards on show at Sheffield United's Hall of Fame.

Looking at the team who faced Gillingham, we had a nice balance in the side. Keith Waugh was a good, steady keeper who cost around £100,000 when we were in the Fourth Division. Mick Henderson was made captain for the day because Paul Stancliffe was feeling his way. Mick was a good player and we got on great. Stancliffe, who came in from Rotherham during the summer, settled in very quickly and became a smashing captain. At right-back we had Bob Atkins who was 'Mr Versatile' and played in various positions. He was a great athlete who could run forever. On the opposite flank, Paul Garner was a smashing lad and a great little player with a neat left foot. In midfield, Kevin Arnott was a bit special and he would thread balls through. He had great vision and, like a snooker player, he was five or six shots in front of everybody else. I learned that as the season went on with Kevin. You couldn't fall-out with Kevin on the pitch because he would get upset about that. I was a whinger and if you shouted at him, he wouldn't give you the ball!

Mike Trusson was a great attacking midfielder who could get up and down the field. Every now and then Truss would play up front and he also did that job well. Ray McHale sat in midfield and fed the ball to Colin Morris. He was better than a water-carrier. I used to say to him, "Don't worry, we're going to get 43 goals between us. All be it, I'm going to score 42 of them…" I ended the season with 33 goals in 44 League appearances to win my second Golden Boot and we won promotion to Division Two after finishing third.

We then started going backwards. When we were in the Fourth Division, we were thinking like a Second Division club and when we were in the Second Division, we started thinking like a Fourth Division club. It was as though we just wanted to try and survive, instead of trying to carry on making progress. We brought in players like Phil Thompson, Peter Withe and Ken McNaught who were at the end of their careers and it didn't work. There were some good players like Peter Nicholas, Ray Houghton and Mick Harford who Ian Porterfield tried to sign and maybe it was the club's fault for not signing them.

After finishing just above the relegation zone in the 1984/85 season, we were seventh at the end of the following campaign. When we had a meeting at the end of the season, someone said, "We're the best team in the division."

I can't cope with comments like that, so I got up and said, "No, we're not, we're the seventh best team in the division." I know exactly what he meant, but the best team in the division finishes top. Jimmy McGuigan, an old Scottish coach who was brought in by Ian Porterfield, summed up my attitude perfectly. He took me to one side in training and said, "Keith, you don't suffer fools and that's the reason why you have a lot of fall-outs."

Spanish club Seville came in for me and Colin Morris. United considered selling me because the fee was right, which once again I was surprised at.

My attitude was, "If you're prepared to sell me, I'm prepared to go." I went with Colin to Spain for a few days and we played in a practice match. We did well in a 3-1 win with Colin scoring twice and me getting the other goal. But the transfer fell through because they had a change of coach.

I did leave, however, in 1986 when I was told that an offer from Leeds for me had been accepted. In my book, once they'd accepted it, there was no point not speaking to the people concerned. I spoke to Leeds and loved manager Billy Bremner right from the start. I thought he was great because he got straight to the point and told me what I was being offered. When I told him what I was after, he went away, sorted it out and asked me if I'd sign. After agreeing to join Leeds, I was disappointed when United claimed in the Press that they'd offered me exactly what Leeds had offered. That was so far from the truth it was unreal because you've got to take into account what you actually make from the transfer itself. They may have offered the same basic salary, but they couldn't match the whole package.

I felt very let down by United because I never instigated the move at all. In saying that, I did feel that Leeds were making a little bit more progress than United and I was proved right. We got to the FA Cup semi-finals and were seven minutes away from winning promotion to the top-flight because we were beating Charlton in the Play-offs. At that time, you played the team third from bottom in the top-flight and we took them to three games after drawing twice. We were the nearly team that year. I thoroughly enjoyed my time at Leeds, but I did go quite a few games without scoring and it took me a bit of time to settle in. I got a lot of important goals for Leeds. The semi-final of the Cup was fantastic, especially as it was at Hillsborough. It was one of the best semi-finals ever and I came on to score and take it to extra-time. I nearly got another one in extra-time.

I felt I had to leave Leeds when it became clear that their style of play didn't suit my game. Billy Bremner explained that he wasn't going to change things around just to accommodate me, agreed to let me go and we parted on great terms. I linked up with Ian Porterfield again at Aberdeen because I thought it would be a good experience. The standard was average in Scotland if you weren't playing Celtic or Rangers and I found it boring, so when Hull came in for me, I decided to go back there. I won my third Golden Boot at the age of 33 after scoring 26 League goals and I rate that as one of my best achievements. I beat Ian Wright and Kerry Dixon to the Golden Boot and Crystal Palace and Chelsea got promoted that season, while we finished fourth from bottom. That summed up my career, the fact that those two won promotion to the top-flight and went on to play for England and yet they didn't score as many goals as me. You get overlooked when you're at a club like Hull City. I could easily feel that I missed out, but I try not to think that way.

My career didn't end on a high. After brief spells at Stockport, Huddersfield and Plymouth, I packed in playing because my hip was killing me. It was knackered and still is. I would have loved to have stayed in the game. I had one little chance which came when I was the senior professional at Hull under Eddie Gray. We got on ever so well and I started taking the kids in training. Unfortunately, Eddie got the sack and nothing materialised. I'm not bitter about it because it's just the way it goes and it obviously wasn't meant to be. I had 17 years in professional football and I won't ever better it. I got my HGV licence, which was paid for by the PFA, and worked with my old mate Joe Bolton for a few years. I have to say that work is very over-rated! I was lost a little, if I'm being honest, after finishing playing.

I was going to watch United on a regular basis before being invited by BBC Radio Sheffield to do some work as a match summariser. My first game was the 4-4 draw against Birmingham in 1996, which was a very exciting match, so there was plenty to talk about. I was chipping in with comments at the wrong time for radio, but things have developed from there and it's good fun. I've been doing it for ten years now and it's great to be able to give my opinion. Sometimes it's well taken and sometimes it's not, but I don't worry about that.

I've also worked for Cancer Research for eight or nine years. It's a pleasant job and a great cause. I did some voluntary work at St Luke's Hospice and ended up getting a job as a fund-raiser, helping the managers out at the various shops, travelling up and down the country. The job fits in with my radio work. I've also done some after-dinners, which have gone quite well.

It's brilliant for United to be back in the Premiership. It's a fantastic stadium, which is getting better and better. They've done tremendously well and I love to see players like Danny Webber because I think he's a wonderful player. The pendulum swings and it's finally swung our way. We've got a little opportunity and only time will tell whether we can grasp it.

BOB BOOKER
MIDFIELDER 1988-1991

BORN 25 January 1958, Watford
SIGNED November 1988 from Brentford
BLADES CAREER 123 games, 13 goals
HONOURS Promotion from Division Two 1989/90, Promotion from Division Three 1988/89
LEFT Free transfer to Brentford, November 1991

A player whose whole-hearted approach to the game earned him cult status at Bramall Lane after overcoming a difficult start to his United career. Plucked from Brentford reserves as a stop-gap signing, Bob initially struggled before winning the fans over with some committed displays. He was a key figure in the back-to-back promotions as Dave Bassett took the Blades back to the top-flight.

Leicester City 2 v Sheffield United 5

League Division Two
Saturday 5 May 1990

Filbert Street
Attendance 21,134

The Blades come from behind to win in style on the last day of the season, sealing promotion to the top-flight after a 14-year absence

Teams

David Pleat	**Managers**	Dave Bassett
Martin Hodge	1	Simon Tracey
(Sub. Paul Reid)		
Ally Mauchlen	2	Colin Hill
(Sub. Gary Fitzpatrick)		
George Parris	3	David Barnes
Tommy Wright	4	Bob Booker
Gary McAllister	5	Chris Wilder
Gary Mills	6	Mark Morris
Paul Ramsey	7	Paul Wood
Tony James	8	Wilf Rostron
Marc North	9	Tony Agana
David Oldfield	10	Brian Deane
		(Sub. Billy Whitehurst)
David Kelly	11	Ian Bryson

Mills 7, North 42	**Scorers**	Wood 16, Deane 20, Agana 36, 82, Rostron 40

Referee: V Callow

IT WAS A fantastic time for me at Bramall Lane and I couldn't have asked for more. It'll always live with me. I'm a Sheffield United fan now and I always will be. As they say, "Once a Blade, always a Blade." I was lucky enough to get one of the Executive Boxes named after me. A lot of people mock me about it, but I'm proud of that it because it's something special to be chosen out of a lot of players to have that honour.

Due to the fact that I wanted to play football and become a footballer, I didn't really support a team as a kid. My dad's step-brother went to Leeds University, so I started going up there to watch games at a time when the likes of Allan Clarke, Eddie Gray and Peter Lorimer were playing for them. If I did follow anyone down south, it was probably Chelsea because my friend supported them. I also watched Watford occasionally as they were on the up at the time, but I wasn't really into supporting a team.

I joined Brentford at the age of 19. I didn't do an apprenticeship because I worked in a factory after leaving school, covering furniture. I got a trial at Brentford through the groundsman, who knew one of the directors. I did OK in a trial match against Brighton, scoring twice. I was playing in the reserves and still working in the factory when Brentford manager Bill Dodgin asked me if I'd like to become a full-time pro. At that time, I was earning around £200-a-week in the factory, which was a lot of money in 1978. I was offered a two-year contract on £60-a-week to join Brentford, which I accepted. After telling my parents about my plans, I remember my mum asking me what I was doing, leaving a trade. "Well, I want to become a footballer," I explained. I signed on the Wednesday and made my debut on the Saturday at Watford, my home town.

After being thrown in at the deep end, I lost my way a little bit after that. I didn't really get into the team and needed games at that level, so I went out on loan to non-league Barnet, under Barry Fry. I did OK there and was called back to Brentford after about six months, scoring a hat-trick on my return. I established myself in the team, playing in various positions. After starting out as a forward, I went to right-back and the centre of midfield.

I then ended up winning the Player of the Year award in the second year of my contract.

I had a great few years at Brentford, but then I suffered a bad knee injury, doing my cruciate ligament, which kept me out for two seasons. I was probably one of the first players to have a major cruciate repair and it should have finished me really. After struggling to get back from that, manager Steve Perryman made it clear I wasn't really in his plans. Sheffield United were in the old Third Division at that time, the same as Brentford. When we faced each other, I was taken off with about a quarter of an hour to go and United ended up winning 4-1.

I knew the United physio, Derek French, because we'd played together for a village team called Bedmond Social, along with Vinnie Jones. I travelled home with 'Frenchy' that night after the game and during the journey I said, "I'd love to play in a team like that Del, you're buzzing." The following week, he rang me up and said, "Harry [Dave Bassett] wants to know if you want to come up to Sheffield United."

"You're having a laugh, aren't you?" I replied.

"No, he wants to sign you."

I was in shock because I couldn't believe it. Dave Bassett had tried to sign me for Wimbledon while he was in charge there, but the Brentford manager at that time, Frank McLintock, told him I wasn't available. Bassett had kept tabs on me and when Simon Webster broke his leg, he wanted a like-for-like replacement in the centre of midfield. I phoned Steve Perryman that night, told him that United wanted me and travelled up to Bramall Lane with my dad the following morning. Just turning up at the ground was a thrill because playing for a club of that size was something I'd always wanted to do. I sat round a table with Bassett and Derek Dooley, who made me a great offer. I was offered a two-year contract, more or less trebling the wages I was on at Brentford. I also received a signing-on fee, which I'd never had before. I signed that day, which was a Wednesday, before returning home.

I drove back to Sheffield the following day and made my debut on the Saturday against Bristol City. I was rusty after being out of the Brentford side and the way Harry had us playing made it difficult for me as well, so I was well off the pace. The fans must have thought, "What the f*** are we doing, signing a 31-year-old player whose knee is f***ed?" It wasn't what I'd expected because the pace of the game was quicker, with the ball being played forward at the earliest opportunity. I competed and that just about got me through it, but I was breathing out of my arse!

I struggled for quite a while, to be honest, but Harry believed in me and I just kept going. I was getting a lot of stick from the crowd before everything just seemed to click into place on a rainy night at Mansfield at the start of April. I got into every challenge, won my headers and started to pass the ball a bit. I felt as if I'd finally slotted into the pattern of play that Harry was playing and it snowballed from there.

My game was all about breaking things up, giving the ball to someone who could do something with it and popping up with the odd goal. I had a good engine and I could run and tackle. The fans really took to me after that performance at Field Mill and the 'Ooh-aah Bob Book-ah' chants started. It was kind of bizarre, but I loved hearing them chant my name and it makes the hairs on the back of my neck stand up, just talking about it. I loved chipping in and having a good rapport with the fans. I worked on it and it made me feel part of Sheffield United. To his credit, a member of the United staff, Mick Rooker, took me around the town, visiting working men's clubs and meeting people. I was up in Sheffield on my own because my wife was still in Watford, so I had loads of time on my hands. I enjoyed going to pubs and clubs to talk to the fans and more players should do that.

When I left Brentford, some people said to me, "What are you going up there for? It's all flat caps and chimneys." But I loved it in Sheffield. Sure, it's a slower pace of life than in London, but everybody tends to know everybody in the area where they live and I found the Sheffield people very friendly. You could walk down the street and people would say "Good Morning" to you. Some of the surrounding areas are fantastic as well. I'm into walking and bird-watching, so I had the best of both worlds; the hustle and bustle of Sheffield and then going out into Derbyshire and the Peak District. I really did enjoy my time in Sheffield and I would have been quite happy to live there permanently. Harry had told me not to buy a house when I first came up to United. He reasoned that with a two-year contract, it wasn't a good idea to lose my house in Watford. I stayed in a hotel for a few months and then drifted around, living with different people including Geoff Taylor, Derek French, Ian Bryson, Chris Wilder and Tony Agana. I had to get out of the digs I was sharing with Geoff, Frenchy and Ian because it was doing my head in! Chris had a house at Gleadless and me, him and Tony lived together there for about eight months.

We won promotion from Division Three at the end of my first season, 1988/89, and when I limped off during the final home game, against Swansea, I received a standing ovation. We started the following campaign with a 3-0 win at West Brom. The BBC were filming a documentary around us during that campaign and, with the way things went, it worked out great for them. It was pretty much between us, Newcastle and Leeds all the way that season.

We were just a team of thugs really and none of the players cost big money. Brian Deane and Tony Agana were both bought on the cheap and we had experienced lads like Mark Morris and Wilf Rostron, so it was a team made up out of nothing. Deane and Agana were just phenomenal and, if you've got two centre-forwards who can score 20-odd goals apiece, you're up, it's as simple as that. We played a percentage game, getting the ball forward to them. Harry always had two wingers and two centre-forwards, so we'd get the ball wide to Bryson, Alan Roberts or Paul Wood, who would get early crosses in for Brian and Tony to feed off. We got some stick for the way we played, but we didn't give a shit what anyone thought. We believed in what we did after doing it day in, day out on the training pitch. Harry was a great believer in a pattern of play which saw us get the ball into an area he called the 'reacher', getting the back-four turned so they were stretched. It was basic, but it worked. It's so similar to what teams do today, but that's not recognised. We're still thought of as a 'long ball' team.

We trained together and socialised together. Harry built that team-spirit and it was part of the reason why we were successful. It was something special and we talk about it when we get together now. Even Harry socialised with us. You knew he was the manager and knew you couldn't cross him, but he'd have a beer with you. Frenchy and the kit man, John Greaves, were also strong characters who the players loved, so we had a team full of characters on the pitch and we also had a team of characters off it as well.

It was mainly good humoured banter between the players, but it could kick off sometimes and get quite nasty. I remember getting a good ragging from some of the northern lads on one occasion at the training ground. It was snowing and I was attacked by several of them including Billy Whitehurst and Dane Whitehouse. They stripped all my training kit off and I was left there, absolutely freezing, so I had to make my way back to the ground in just my slip!

Billy was a fantastic character and a great example for any young centre-forward who wanted to learn how to shield the ball and head it. It was a great bit of management by Harry to sign Billy at the back end of the season. We'd be 2-0 up and Billy would come on as a sub for Deane or Agana to give defenders a fresh problem to think about. Billy's a fantastic bloke and someone you'd want with you in the trenches.

Sometimes after we'd suffered a defeat, Harry would order us in for training the following day. If he knew that I hadn't been home for a month, he'd take me to one side and tell me that I could go back down south. I'd get called 'Son of Dave' by the other lads, but that's what he was like. He knew how to man-manage and that's a massive part of the job. It should also be remembered that so much of our success was down to the coach, Geoff Taylor as well. Most days in training, Geoff would be doing everything and Dave would come up later on to put the finishing touches. They were the perfect pair, bouncing off each other. I know from my experience, working with the likes of Steve Coppell, Peter Taylor and Micky Adams, that a manager and his coach have to become a pair and there has to be a lot of trust there. It's almost like being married, but to a bloke! If you can get that mix working, then you're flying. Geoff was totally devoted to his job and football was his life. He was hard but fair and all the lads loved him. I owe him a lot and still keep in touch with him now. When I went back to Brentford, he came in as youth team director and I was a coach under him.

We had a couple of blips towards the end of the season, losing 4-0 at Leeds and 5-0 at West Ham. After the West Ham game some people questioned whether we had enough left in the tank to win a second successive promotion. I played alongside Mark Morris in central defence that night and we were slaughtered afterwards by Harry who called us 'a couple of donkeys'. We won on Oldham's plastic pitch the following week, but I didn't play in that game because my knee wouldn't have stood up to playing on the artificial surface. We then drew our penultimate match at Blackburn. Whitehurst could have sealed promotion for us when he had a chance with a far post header.

Going into the last day at Leicester, we were level on points with Leeds, but they had a superior goal difference. We knew that a victory at Filbert Street would take us up. If we failed to win, we'd be sweating on the games involving Leeds and Newcastle, who were playing at Bournemouth and Middlesbrough respectively. With Paul Stancliffe missing through injury, I was handed the captain's armband. I didn't expect it, to be honest, because we had Chris Wilder, who was a Sheffield lad, but Harry informed me I was to be captain for the day. It was a real honour, especially with the pressure of the game, and leading the team out did give it an added edge for me. There had been pre-match talk of me going back to central defence to replace Stancliffe because I'd played on a number of occasions in that position, but Harry kept me in midfield and drafted in Colin Hill to play at the back.

I can remember travelling on the coach through the streets surrounding Filbert Street, seeing all the United fans there. It was a very upbeat coach; no-one was just sitting there quietly. I know it's easy to say after all these years that we knew we were going to win, but we just didn't have any fear. We knew what was at stake and we were very confident. We just thought, "Let's go for it." Seeing all the fans and hearing them singing our names made it feel just like a home game. Leicester had nothing to play for really, so we had to go and do the business. Before we ran out onto the pitch, Harry said that we all knew what was at stake and we had to go out and compete for 90 minutes. Looking at the TV footage from that day, I think Harry was probably more nervous than us. Us players were all pretty low-key about it because the preparation had been done.

As we came out of the tunnel, we saw that the top and bottom levels of the stand were full of Blades. Hundreds of them were wearing the famous luminous yellow shirt, which was probably the best-selling shirt in Umbro's history. It seemed like everybody else was in fancy dress, wearing all sorts of costumes.

Gary Mills gave Leicester an early lead, scoring in the ninth minute. We just all looked at each other and said, "F***ing hell, let's go for it now." Paul Wood equalised following a cross from Ian Bryson and then Brian Deane put us in front. I'll never forget that goal because the ball took forever to go into the net. There were loads of ricochets and goalkeeper Martin Hodge got hit in the mouth before Deano turned it in. All the players jumped on top of Deano and I was above them, trying to do the captain's bit, calming everyone down.

To add to the mayhem, we also had the fans in fancy dress coming onto the pitch as well. They came onto it every time we scored a goal. We were trying the get them off the pitch and suddenly you'd find yourself stood next to a character like Mickey Mouse or a pantomime horse. It was unbelievable. That sort of thing wouldn't happen nowadays because the game would get stopped. Players are even getting booked for going up to the barrier to celebrate with their own supporters, but you look back to that day at Leicester and there was no trouble despite all those people flooding onto the pitch.

Tony Agana made it 3-1 with a volley following a back header from Deane. In the Leicester goal, Hodge was still groggy after being struck in the melée leading up to our second goal and he didn't react when Wilf Rostron fired in a slow, left-foot shot, which flew across the goal and into the net. Hodge was clearly struggling and he had to go off soon afterwards.

We had got in their faces in the first-half and upset them. In the mood we were in, I don't think there are many teams who'd have coped with us. I was marking Gary McAllister, who was a key figure for them. I respected him as a player because he was a legend, but he obviously didn't know who I was. When I got booked after challenging him, the United fans started chanting my name. I remember McAllister looking up and saying, "What the f*** are they singing your name for?" Staring straight back at him, I replied, "Because I'm Ooh-aah Bob Book-ah!"

Marc North scored Leicester's second in first-half injury time to make it 4-2 at the break, which was a dangerous score. If we conceded the next goal we'd be in the position of hanging onto a single goal lead after having lead by three clear goals, but we were still confident of finishing the job off. In the BBC TV series, Bassett and Taylor were shown arguing about tactics at half-time. We were sat there thinking, "What the f*** are they going on about, we're cruising." When Leicester did manage to find a way through in the second-half, Simon Tracey kept them out. 'Trace' was a sloppy trainer, the world's worst, but put him in a match situation and he was fantastic.

Agana got his second goal of the match and our fifth when he capitalised on a mistake from George Parris, breaking away and slipping the ball under North. That was effectively game over. Once the final whistle went, we ran off down the tunnel before Paul Stancliffe, as club captain, led the players back onto the pitch. I had wanted him to lead us out before the game, but that wasn't allowed because his name wasn't on the team-sheet. The plan was to come back on and do a lap of honour, but that wasn't going to happen because so many fans had flooded onto the pitch. Dave Bassett ended up being stripped down to his slip on the pitch and fans carried him around on their shoulders.

With Sheffield Wednesday suffering relegation from the First Division that same day, Blades fans were singing, "United up, Wednesday down." It was fantastic. I was 32 and never thought I'd play in the First Division. It was great to get promotion, which was the main thing, but it would have been nice to have won the title as well. We just missed out on that honour, though, as Leeds won at Bournemouth to clinch the Championship. The only team who could have denied us promotion on that dramatic final day, Newcastle, lost 4-1 at Middlesbrough and then went out of the play-offs by losing at home to Sunderland. I can't imagine what that must have felt like. Winning promotion definitely felt unbelievable!

I remember walking towards my car after the game with my dad and my sister, carrying a four-pack of beer under my arm. (You wouldn't encourage players to drink alcohol straight after a game nowadays, but that's what we did then; we worked hard and played hard). There was a big queue of traffic coming out of the car park and fans were reaching out of their car windows to shake my hand. I headed straight back to Watford because my family had all come up and I hadn't been home for about a month, but I wished I'd have gone back to Bramall Lane to join in the celebrations with the rest of the lads.

We lost 3-1 at home to Liverpool in our opening game in Division One in a game in which Simon Tracey was injured and John Pemberton had to take over in goal. Time was running out for me and I didn't expect to play that much because my knee was knackered, but it was just nice to get a chance to turn out in the top-flight. I knew I wasn't going to get another contract, but at least I'd got there and played a part in that first season which saw us established in the top flight, which was good enough for me.

At the end of the season I discussed my future with Harry and he couldn't really offer me anything more due to my age and the way my knee was. Brentford had come in with an offer to take me back there on a two-and-a-half-year contract. I was torn really because I didn't want to go, but Harry could only offer me a year-long deal, which I wanted to take, but I needed a bit of security. In the end, after weighing everything up, I made the harsh decision to leave Sheffield and return to Brentford.

We played newly promoted Sheffield Wednesday at that time and Harry told me that he wanted me to go out at half-time and do a lap of honour. "You're having a laugh," I said. But he was insistent. "You go out there, you deserve it." So I went out and it was a very moving moment when the fans applauded me and chanted my name, especially being in such a big game. I had a lump in my throat and I'll never forget it. I came back up and sat with the fans for the return derby match at Hillsborough and got the singing going. Despite having left the club, I'd come up for games whenever I could and I loved it.

I had to retire from playing when my knee finally packed up. It came as a bit of a shock because you're left wondering what to do after being in football for most of your life. I drifted around for a bit and played in non-league football. During a year out of the professional game, I went on some coaching courses and then received a phone call from Brentford, asking me to go back there once again, this time as youth team coach. I later moved up to work with the reserves under Micky Adams, who took me to Brighton as his assistant when he joined the Seagulls.

I ended up working under a few managers at Brighton. I don't think I'll become a manager myself because I enjoy the coaching role I'm doing. I had a little taste of being a manager when I took over as caretaker-boss. It's not that I didn't enjoy the pressure, but sometimes you get the feeling it's not for you. As coach I'm closer to the players, acting as the manager's eyes, and it was hard to mix the two when I was caretaker-manager. I found that very difficult, so once I knew that I wasn't going to be getting the job, I had to tell the chairman that because I didn't want to lose my role working with the players. I experienced three promotions with Brighton and two relegations, which hurt, so now, after leaving the club when Mark McGhee was sacked in 2006, I'm looking to bounce back.

I had a T-shirt hanging up in the kit room at Brighton with my caricature and 'Ooh-aah Bob Book-ah' written on it. Everybody thought it was Eric Cantona's chant, but it was officially mine. The Leeds United fans heard the Blades fans chanting my name when we played them – and only then did they start singing, 'Ooh-aah Cantona.' Never let a Leeds fan tell you otherwise. They stole it from us.

I went to a dinner in honour of Dave Bassett when he left his home in Sheffield to return south and that was a fantastic night. All the lads wanted to go and support the man after what he did for us. I have a lot to thank both Dave and Derek Dooley for because they really looked after me. There are a lot of people still there behind the scenes at Bramall Lane from my time. They include the likes of Andy Daykin, Andy Pack and Mick Rooker, who've stuck by the club. I speak to Mick most weeks and he keeps me in touch with what's going on there. I'm just glad United are back in the Premiership and I hope they can stay there because it's where they deserve to be. It's a great football club, with a great stadium, in a great city.

DANE WHITEHOUSE
MIDFIELDER 1989–1999

BORN   14 October 1970, Sheffield
SIGNED   July 1989, from Apprentice
BLADES CAREER   269 games 48 goals
HONOURS   Promotion from Division Two 1989/90, Promotion from Division Three 1988/89
LEFT   Retired due to injury, 1999

A Sheffield-born left-sided midfielder whose direct style and whole-hearted attitude made him a popular figure. A total of three goals against Sheffield Wednesday ensured his place in Blades folklore. Dane pledged his loyalty to the club by rejecting a lucrative offer from Birmingham before seeing his career cruelly ended by injury when he was in his prime.

Sheffield Wednesday 1 v Sheffield United 3

League Division One
Wednesday 11 March 1992

Hillsborough
Attendance 40,327

Blades complete a memorable double over a Wednesday side bound for Europe

Teams

Trevor Francis	**Managers**	Dave Bassett
Chris Woods	1	Simon Tracey
Roland Nilsson	2	Kevin Gage
Phil King	3	David Barnes
Carlton Palmer	4	John Gannon
Viv Anderson	5	Brian Gayle
Peter Shirtliff	6	Paul Beesley
Danny Wilson	7	Carl Bradshaw
(Sub .Nigel Jemson)		
Graham Hyde	8	Paul Rogers
David Hirst	9	Bobby Davison
		(Sub .Alan Cork)
Paul Williams	10	Brian Deane
Nigel Pearson	11	Dane Whitehouse
(Sub. John Harkes)		(Sub. Glyn Hodges)
King 49	**Scorers**	Whitehouse 4, Davison 28, 67

Referee: R Hart

I'VE ALWAYS FOLLOWED Sheffield United and I was lucky enough to be taken on by them when I was a kid. I've got a step-brother who took me to my first game in November 1979 when we beat Gillingham 4-0. I also went to the 'Boxing Day Massacre' that season with my dad who's a big United fan. I lived at Woodthorpe and went to Brook School, which is no longer there, but I was always playing football.

I played for Sheffield Boys from the under-11s to the under-14s and moved from Sheffield Rangers to the Junior Blades. At the age of 13 or 14, you get all the scouts coming to watch you and that's when it starts getting more serious. It's all changed now because they're getting picked up at about eight years-old, but in those days it wasn't until you were about 13 or 14 that clubs signed you up on schoolboy forms. Trials were held during the school holidays and you'd go to every single club in the area. I went to United, Wednesday, Rotherham, Barnsley and Chesterfield. United were more interested in me than the other clubs and they had probably the best set-up, so I joined.

United scout John Stubbs was based in Mosborough and it was him who picked me up. I used to go to a School of Excellence one day a week, which was in the old gym behind the South Stand at Bramall Lane. In the holidays, we went to Westfield School for coaching. You were then told whether you were being taken on or not.

When I started my apprenticeship on a YTS scheme, the United manager was Billy McEwan. He was there for the first couple of months before being sacked and then Dave Bassett came in towards the end of my first year. My ideal role was playing on the left-hand side of midfield, pushing on, but as I progressed and got stronger, I played at left-back quite a bit. I admit that I wasn't good at defending, but I got better after being moved into a defensive position. I even played at centre-half for a number of games in the juniors, under Keith Mincher. They used to move you into different positions to improve your knowledge of the game. Dave Bassett did that with a lot of players. Mitch Ward, for example, was an out and out right-winger, but he played many times at right-back. It was the same with Carl Bradshaw, who was a centre-forward before being moved to right-wing and later right-back. Under Bassett, wingers were tucked in and had to defend more and then get forward and attack more. You were given licence to use the flank to your advantage.

I missed most of United's first season back in the top-flight due to a knee ligament injury. The following season, we faced Sheffield Wednesday after they'd won promotion back to the First Division after suffering relegation the same day we'd won promotion in 1989. We hadn't played them in a competitive fixture for a number of years, so there was a lot of hype in the build-up to the first game, which was at our place. Because we were at the bottom of the table and Wednesday were riding high, they came to Bramall Lane with thoughts of absolutely stuffing us. As a lad who'd grown up on a so-called rough estate in Sheffield, where half my mates were United fans and the other half were Wednesday fans, the game had extra significance for me. I used to have a bit of banter with my mates who were Wednesday fans, but they used to say to me that whatever happened, they always wanted me to do well because I'd done well for the estate.

Realistically, we shouldn't have got a result out of the game, but we seemed to want it more than they did. It showed in the game, which I've watched on video loads of times. We were all over them and I was lucky enough to score in a 2-0 win. What I was very good at was to get myself in positions to either finish off a scoring opportunity myself or set-up someone else to score.

When the return derby game came round, we didn't have a game on the Saturday before the midweek game at Hillsborough, so Dave Bassett took us up to Scotland for the week. With a big game coming up like that, the build-up starts a week or so before, with all the media coming down to the training ground. It tends to get on top of you, so we needed to get away from our normal environment. We were based in Forfar where we trained and played golf. We went out for a couple of drinks, but Bassett was always strict on things like that. A friendly against Kilmarnock was arranged on the Friday, but it was abandoned due to a heavy downpour which left the pitch waterlogged when we were 1-0 down.

After returning from Scotland, Bassett sorted out some tickets for us to watch Wednesday's game at home to Coventry on the Saturday. It wasn't a very nice experience because we received just a little abuse from the home fans! It was good to see how they played and who you were going to be up against. We took along notebooks and jotted down the strengths and weaknesses of the players, so you could use the information to your advantage. You normally see players at eye-level, so it's good to be able to judge them from the stand. I was looking at Wednesday's right-back Roland Nilsson because I knew I'd be up against him if I was selected. But we didn't know who was going to be in the team to face Wednesday, so Ian Bryson and Glyn Hodges were also watching Nilsson. All three of us were sat there, discussing Nilsson's strengths and weaknesses, each hoping we'd be the one to face him. On the Monday morning, we had an hour-long team meeting which gave us each a chance to offer our opinions. That sort of thing also happened on other occasions.

Simon Tracey was a fixture in goal until Alan Kelly came to the club. You'd want either of those two in your team because they were both world-class keepers. We always did well with keepers because we also had Mel Rees. He had some blinding games before getting injured and then seeing cancer take over. I was so sorry to see the disease claim his life in 1993 because he was a fantastic bloke.

Kevin Gage was a good right-back who weighed-in with a few goals, while David Barnes was solid on the other side of defence. Brian Gayle seemed as though he was hewn from rock in the centre alongside Paul Beesley, who was a good player and a lot stronger than he looked. John Gannon was a midfield maestro. Everything went through him in midfield. He also took the free-kicks and corners. Carl Bradshaw gave his all for the club and Paul Rogers did well after coming from non-league football. Brian Deane is a legend who scored so many goals. Brian likes his own space and he's as quiet as a mouse.

We'd needed more cover in attack, so Dave Bassett brought in a couple of experienced strikers in Alan Cork and Bobby Davison in time for this particular game. Bobby started the match, while 'Corky' was on the bench. We were getting established in mid-table after winning a few games, while Wednesday were going for Europe. The game was probably a bit more intense than the one at Bramall Lane because they wanted revenge. It was an absolutely amazing experience to run out in front of a sell-out 40,000 crowd at Hillsbrough.

I scored after just four minutes to give us the lead. The way we played, we got the ball forward quickly. I was on the left-hand side and I saw Paul Rogers going down the right. I'd played against Roland Nilsson a couple of times and, after watching him the previous Saturday, I knew that I'd got the beating of him in and around the box because I could get that extra yard. So I edged forward, while Roland seemed to be holding back. He didn't seem to be thinking, "the ball is going to be in our box and my player might score here." Roger Nilsen chipped the ball over their defence, Brian Deane got on the end of it and I thought, "I'm in here." Roland was at the side of me, but I managed to hold him off and then he was nowhere to be seen because he'd stopped on the edge of the penalty area. He'd let me run into the box because he didn't think the ball was going to come across, so now the ball was coming across to me and I had an open goal. I saw keeper Chris Woods go to the near post and all I had to do was put my foot through it. The ball was at crawling pace across the face of goal and I'd have gone mad if I'd missed it because I could have put a hat on it! When you have time to think about things like that it's always worrying. All sorts of things go through your head because you know you should score. I thought at one point that I was off-side because there was no-one around me.

After the ball went into the net, I ran round the side of the goal, stuck my hand up to the fans and looked over to the linesman to see if I was off-side. Then I saw the fans jumping all over each other and thought, "That's it, I've scored." Dave Bassett used to say, "Always gamble because you never know when that ball will come across to you." He used to show us videos of games and no end of times the ball would go across the face of goal after missing the strikers and the player following up on the far post had an open goal. We practised running in at the back stick and it worked for me because I scored a lot in that area. It was the same for Carl Bradshaw and Mitch Ward. Because of our width we whipped a lot of crosses across and we knew it was a decent gamble to expect chances to crop up.

Our second goal came when Carl Bradshaw put a long cross into the box and Bobby Davison challenged Chris Woods for a 50/50 ball. It seemed as though Woods had pulled out of it, probably thinking he was going to get hurt, so the ball bounced up onto Bobby's chest and he turned it into the empty net. We were 2-0 up after half an hour, which was unbelievable. Wednesday fans had been saying they were going to get their revenge and they were riding high in the league while we had only recently escaped the relegation zone. Taking all that into account, it was a dream come true.

Wednesday came back into the game soon after half-time when Phil King scored in the 49th minute. I conceded a free-kick on the edge of the box by bringing down Carlton Palmer. The resulting shot from King went through the wall, which blocked Simon Tracey's view. After being 2-0 up and cruising, we'd conceded a goal early in the second-half, leaving us thinking, "Hold on a minute, we're just going to get bombarded here." Wednesday had come from behind to win or draw in each of their previous three home games, including that match against Coventry we'd seen, and that made us a little wary. There was a spell when we were under a lot of pressure because Wednesday were pushing forward, trying to get an equaliser. But that left space for us and we created several chances before scoring our third goal.

Dave Bassett had told us before the game that we needed to get a lot of crosses in and we played some decent balls into the box that night. It was raining and I can remember John Gannon putting over a teasing centre which bent in on goal and Bobby Davison's diving header skidded off the wet turf and into the bottom corner of the net. That was late in the game, so it knocked the stuffing out of them.

To do the double over Wednesday was fantastic. They could have won the League title if we hadn't taken six points off them because they weren't far off champions Leeds.

We weren't the best team technically in the League, but Dave Bassett got the best out of players. We used to get results and that's the bottom line. Bassett's strength was to see what ability a player had got and emphasise that more than any weak points. Bob Booker, for example, wasn't the best player you'd ever seen, but he was in the team near enough every week. That was due to his enthusiasm, his rapport with the fans and the fact that he put 110 per cent in. It takes all sorts to make a real team and Harry was brilliant at putting a bunch of players like us together and creating a sum greater than the parts.

Vinny Jones was a better player than what people thought, but his game was based on his aggression. In the changing room, he used to wind and wind everybody up. We used to bang on the walls before we went out. As we prepared to face the likes of Liverpool and Manchester United, we'd be saying to each other, "Don't get intimated by them, don't look at them." When we saw the opposition players in the tunnel, we'd growl at them to see how strong they were and find out whether they wanted to match us on the pitch. Some of them would look us in the eye and say, "Yeah, we're up for it." But others – and I'm talking some big teams as well – never looked at us in the tunnel.

We went out feeling we'd never get stuffed. As soon as we kicked-off, we'd give our opponents a dig and see if they wanted it for 90 minutes. That's the type of team we were. When other managers came in after Dave Bassett left, we had some better players like Don Hutchison and David White. But if you played Bassett's side against Howard Kendall's side, I don't know who'd win. Under Kendall, we had aggression and passion, but we also had a little bit of flair as well. Mostly under Bassett, it was a case of just getting a result, even if it meant that games didn't look nice.

When you came back for pre-season training, you could guarantee there would be six or seven new players. By the end of the first training session, someone would have been in the changing room and cut the new players' socks up and things like that. It was just a way of saying, "Welcome to the club." All sorts of things like that went on. I can remember a time when Carl Bradshaw and I broke Dave Bassett's ribs during a pre-season trip to Scandinavia. 'Harry' – as we always called Bassett – got onto the coach after having a few drinks with Derek Dooley. He came to the back of the coach where I was sat with 'Brads' and Mitch Ward. "Right, you three Sheffield lads, come on, let's have it," he said. So we pinned him down and started punching him in the ribs. We were only messing about, but he woke up next morning with three cracked ribs! At the team-meeting that morning, Harry started swearing at us.

"You've broken my f***ing ribs!"

"Well, you shouldn't come to the back of the coach, Harry, showing off," we said.

He loved it because he wouldn't have done it otherwise. When you're a young lad mixing with older players, you need to be on the same level. There's no use sitting in a corner and hiding away. You had to show a bit of bottle, otherwise you would have got picked on. It wasn't a case of being bullied or anything like that. It was just that if you shy away in training with the lads, then you're going to shy away on the pitch in the heat of a battle. We were in it together, so if someone was on the receiving end of a nasty tackle, it wasn't just one player running up and having a go at the other bloke, it was all ten outfield players. That's why we used to have rumbles on the pitch, with ten-man brawls.

I broke my right leg against Bristol City in the FA Cup during the 1992/93 season and spent six months out. I made my comeback against Blackburn in the quarter-finals of the FA cup and also played in the semi-final against Wednesday at Wembley. You look back on that day and say that realistically, we shouldn't have conceded a goal from the position Chris Waddle scored from. But the one player who could have scored from there at that time was Waddle. He had lit up the Premiership since returning from his time in France with Marseilles. It was a fantastic atmosphere, but on the day we weren't good enough, it's as simple as that. If it wasn't for Alan Kelly making some fantastic saves, it could have been three or four.

When Howard Kendall came in to replace Dave Bassett after we'd been cruelly relegated on the last day of the 1993/94 season, it was great for the club to have attracted someone of that stature because he'd been at the top, winning various trophies with Everton and managing abroad. When there's a change of management, it's like starting your career again because you've got to try and impress the new manager. In Bassett's last game, against Huddersfield, I broke three ribs, so I didn't play in the first few games under Kendall.

My first game back was against Arsenal at Highbury in the Cup. We beat them 1-0 in the replay at Bramall Lane following a goal from Carl Veart. Kendall was given money to spend and he brought a lot of new players in, which seemed to work. There were players like David White, Michel Vonk, Don Hutchison and Jan-Aage Fjortoft. All of a sudden we were riding high, looking to get promotion again. We reached the 1997 Play-off final against Crystal Palace. On paper, we had a far stronger squad than Palace, but we didn't play well. In fact, neither team played well that day. Palace's David Hopkin struck a shot from nowhere with the last kick of the game. He was hoping for the best and it flew into the top corner.

Howard Kendall returned to Everton that summer and was replaced by his assistant, Nigel Spackman. I was on holiday in Tenerife with my mates when my dad called me on my mobile phone. He told me that it was in the papers that I'd been sold to Birmingham. "How can I have been sold to Birmingham when I'm sat on a beach in Tenerife?" I replied.

"Well, that's what it says in the paper," he said.

"I can't do anything about it now – I'll have to see what happens when I go back to Bramall Lane."

When I returned home from holiday, I picked up a message on my mobile phone from the United Chief Executive Charles Green, asking me to report to his office on the Monday morning. Green was a hatchet-man type and a lot of people didn't like him, but he was a businessman. One of his quotes was, "If I could make more money by growing potatoes on that field, I would do." When I went to see Green, he explained that Birmingham had come in with a bid. "We think it's reasonable enough and we've accepted it, but you need to go and see Nigel Spackman," Green said.

I always believe in being able to speak to someone man-to-man, so I went to Nigel's office and had a chat with him. "I understand the club has accepted an offer, but it's all down to you," I said. "Am I going to be in your plans for the coming season?"

"You're in my plans, so I don't want you to go," he said.

"Well, that's fine by me, I'll turn the offer down."

If Nigel had told me that I wouldn't be playing that year, then that might have been time to go. I think people would have understood that. I went back to Charles Green and told him that Nigel was happy for me to stay at the club. Green then apparently got straight on the phone to Birmingham manager Trevor Francis and told him that I didn't want to go there because I thought they were a rubbish team and that I had a better chance with United that season!

Francis phoned me at home and tried to get me to change my mind by offering me a lot of money. But I told him straight that I wasn't interested. "Trevor, I'll tell you the truth, as it is. Thank you for the opportunity, but the reason I turned you down is because I spoke to Nigel personally and he has told about me the plans he'd got and the players he was signing. I think we've got a good chance of getting promoted. I feel as though I can do things at United."

"Cheers for telling me," Francis replied. "Thanks for being honest, but I'll offer you..." He then came up with an increased figure and, as a further incentive, said I could even still live in Sheffield and travel down. It was tempting, but I stood firm, insisting I wasn't going to change my mind. I think my attitude surprised Francis. "To be honest, I've never come across a player like you," he said. "Players would jump at the chance to move when that sort of money is involved. I think you're a great player and I think you're an honest kid who talks from the heart. If anything changes, give me a bell." He then explained that he'd tried to sign me along with Brian Deane when he was at Sheffield Wednesday. Dave Bassett had responded to the enquiry by saying, "Trevor, don't even think about it because neither of them will go." He was right because there was no chance of me ever signing for Wednesday. Even if I'd left United to play abroad, wanted to come back to play in this country and the only choice I'd got was to go to Wednesday, I wouldn't have done it.

Under Kendall, we had played a 4-4-2 formation, but Spackman switched me inside, as he used three at the back with five in midfield. I tucked in and really enjoyed playing in that role because I got forward a lot more. I had 'Hutch' and Mark Patterson alongside me, so they used to give me leeway to run into the box more and help the forwards out. I scored eight or nine goals and we were riding high at the top of the league when I suffered the injury that ended my career. It was in the match at Port Vale following a challenge from Gareth Ainsworth. I can remember it as if it just happened yesterday. Early on in the game, I received a ball from Mitch Ward which over-ran just in front of me. I had caught Roger Nilsen in the corner of my eye when I saw this player coming for me, running straight forward. I just played the ball to Roger and was then caught on the knee. I knew straight away it was a serious injury because I felt it pop, crack and twist and I was in absolute agony. I've broken my leg, ribs and jaw, but nothing compares to what I went through with that. I snapped both my anterior and posterior cruciate ligaments, which is what I felt initially. When the physio came over to attend to me, I told him that I'd done my knee.

I went to see the specialist the following day and, on the Monday morning, I was operated on. I asked the surgeon what my chances of playing again were.

"It's going to be a real battle," he said.

"Well, I'm fit enough and strong enough. I've never given in to anything. If you want a battle on your hands, then you've certainly got one."

"I'd rate your chances at fifty per cent."

"Well, fifty per cent is enough for me."

I could tell there were doubts in his mind and there were doubts in the physio's mind as well, but they let me get on with it. I was so disappointed when people later came up to me and said, "I've heard off the surgeon that you'll never get back to playing."

"Who are you to say that to me?" I'd say to them. "He's got no right to tell you that."

That made me even more determined because I knew that people were doubting me. It was a long road back, working in the gym seven days a week, from nine o'clock in the morning until five o'clock at night. I did a lot of upper-body weights and leg weights and got really solid, but I needed to get out to do my cardio stuff because by now I was built like a body-builder. I went through hell to eventually get back and managed to play six reserve games.

The only reason I packed in was because, in training one day, when I was not under any pressure, I went to control a ball and my knee gave way on the inside. The damage had orignally occured on the outside of the knee and at the back. I asked the physio why it was giving way on the inside. He iced the knee and told me to take a week off training. I felt fine after the break, apart from a few twinges every so often, which is natural because it can take months to recover from an injury. But then in my first training session after coming back, I was just running down the wing when a ball came across and my knee gave way as I went to control it. I took my training bib off and said, "That's it. If I can't even control a ball, what's going to happen if someone comes flying through me? I'm going to let myself down and let the team down."

If you're not 100 per cent fit, there's no point pushing on. I'd had two operations on my knee and the more operations you have, the worse it gets. I also had to think about what would happen in ten years time. I had a chat with the specialist and told him that I didn't want to end up a cripple. I was 29 or 30, coming up to my prime, and had to decide whether I wanted to pinch another two or three years out of the game, with the possibility of hurting myself. Alternatively, I could enjoy the rest of my life, knowing full well that I could go in the park and have a kick-about with my kids or whatever. I could also do things like go to the gym and play golf instead of crippling myself.

I still get a lot of pain and I've got a large scar around my knee, but at least I'm active. I play golf regularly and enjoy my life now.

I took a year out, maybe even a year-and-a-half, after packing in playing and did nothing. I got away from football completely and went away for a couple of months. It gave me a chance to get out of the limelight and think about what I wanted to do. I then went to do my coaching qualification and when Neil Warnock took over as manager, I was at a stage in my life where I needed to know what I was going into. I wasn't receiving a wage and I had a mortgage to pay. Even though I'd put money away during my career, it wasn't going to last forever. I wanted to do some coaching and after being told by United that I'd always be looked after and that there was a job for life for me, I came back to the club. The only job they could offer me at that time, however, was a part-time coaching role, which was on a Tuesday night, a Thursday night and one Sunday in every month. I said, "Well, it's a start and you've got to start somewhere." But I then found out that it was just £25 a session. The other coaches all had full-time jobs and they were doing the coaching in their spare time. After coming out of football, I didn't have a full-time job and £50-a-week didn't even pay a food bill, never mind anything else. I told Neil Warnock that I couldn't accept the offer. "Well, you've got to start somewhere," he said.

"I can understand that, but I've got a mortgage and bills to pay. Look, thanks, but no thanks."

I then totally moved away from football altogether. I had a lot of spare time on my hands, so I did some work for a couple of mates who'd got a courier business. When they got work in they couldn't do themselves, I'd get a phone call asking what I was doing that day. "I haven't got anything planned," I'd say.

"Do you fancy going down London? I need a parcel taking down to London and there's a hundred quid there."

I enjoyed the work and I was earning some decent money. I sat down with a couple of the lads who were doing courier work and found out more about the job. "If you go self-employed, all you need is a van, insurance and customer base and you're well away," I was told. "Surely, you must know so many people, Dane. If people knew what you were going into, then they'd use you left, right and centre." That's what's happened. I've now got a contract with a flower company, delivering to various shops, which means early starts. I have to get up at about 3.30am to go down to Parkway Market from Monday to Saturday, but I enjoy it. Most days I'm back home by about 11.30am. I've got other contracts as well and do a lot for Sheffield University, getting passports stamped for the lecturers.

I enjoy going down to Bramall Lane now as a fan. There's nothing finer than going to The Cricketers or The Sportsman before the game and having a couple of pints, watching the game and then having a couple of pints afterwards. I think I've got a better rapport with the fans now than when I was playing because you don't tend to see them when you're a player. I've got a season ticket in the South Stand and I enjoy going to the games with my mates who I grew up with. There have been people around me throughout my life who are still there now. But there are also others, who were around me when I was a footballer, who are not there now. I've sussed them out and realised they were only there for one thing.

The return of Premiership football has been a long time coming. It's going to be difficult and we need to be on the top of our game every single week. Financially, the club is on a massive footing and we're moving in the right direction. We've got a big academy and there are various projects on the go, so all of a sudden, we're one of the biggest teams in the region and coming up to being one of the biggest in the country.

ALAN KELLY
GOALKEEPER 1992–1999

BORN   11 August 1968, Preston
SIGNED   July 1992 from Preston North End; £200,000
BLADES CAREER   253 games
HONOURS   34 Republic of Ireland caps, 1 Republic of Ireland U23
cap, 3 Republic of Ireland U21 caps
LEFT   Transferred to Blackburn Rovers, July 1999; £675,000

A solid, reliable goalkeeper who rarely made errors. During Alan's seven-
year spell at the Lane, Simon Tracey was his main rival for the first-team
jersey and there was little to choose between the pair. Alan had a superb
temperament and performed particularly well in big games.

Sheffield United 1 v Coventry City 1

after extra time; United won 3-1 on penalties

FA Cup Sixth Round replay
Tuesday 17 March 1998

Bramall Lane
Attendance 29,034

Blades secure Cup semi-final spot following a dramatic penalty shoot-out

Teams

Steve Thompson	**Managers**	Gordon Strachan
Alan Kelly	1	Steve Ogrizovic
Chris Short	2	Roland Nilsson
(Sub. Petr Katchouro)		
Roger Nilsen	3	David Burrows
Vas Borbokis	4	George Boateng
Lee Sandford	5	Dion Dublin
David Holdsworth	6	Gary Breen
Bobby Ford	7	Paul Telfer
Nicky Marker	8	Trond Soltvedt
		(Sub. Gavin Strachan)
Gareth Taylor	9	Noel Whelan
Marcelo	10	Viorel Moldovan
(Sub. Lee Morris)		(Sub. Simon Haworth)
Wayne Quinn	11	Darren Huckerby
Holdsworth 90	**Scorers**	Telfer 10

Referee: S Dunn

As I WOKE from my slumber, Carl Bradshaw was staring at me and David Barnes had me in a headlock; they said they wanted a fight. It was an unusual way to greet a new team-mate!

We were on a coach heading to London after I'd linked up with the United squad for the first time. I thought they were messing about, but the next minute Brads was biting my head and Barnesy was ripping my new Sheffield United shirt off. I thought, "Sod this," and decided to retaliate. "Come on then," I said, squaring up to them. They were both up for it and Barnesy shouted, "Punch me," as he came towards me. I hit him and he fell down the steps leading to the toilet in the middle of the coach. I thought I was in trouble, but Barnesy just got up and said, "Fantastic! Like that. Welcome to Sheffield United!"

I started out as an electrician at Leyland Motors, spending 18 months there at the same time as playing for Preston reserves. It came to the crunch and I had to choose between a career in football or working as an electrician. My dad, also called Alan Kelly, had played in goal for Preston, appearing in their 1964 FA Cup final defeat to West Ham, and later had a spell there as manager, and he wanted me to learn a trade. But I was adamant that I wanted to play football, so I signed as a professional for Preston in September 1985 and made my debut the following February. In my first season we were re-elected after finishing second from bottom in the old Division Four. But the following season we won promotion, so it was an interesting start to my career.

After seven years at Preston, my transfer to United came about very quickly. I went to First Division Notts County on loan in 1992 for two weeks. Neil Warnock was the manager there and I was going to sign for them, but things didn't quite work out. I was in my car on the way back home to Preston when Dave 'Harry' Bassett rang me and asked if I wanted to sign for Sheffield United. I said "Yes" straight away. Harry told me I'd get £25-a-week more than I was on at Preston before asking, "You've just got married, haven't you?"

"Yes, two weeks ago," I confirmed.

"Make that fifty," he added.

I didn't have an agent, so there were no lengthy negotiations and the call must have only lasted about two minutes. I was told to report the following morning for a pre-season tour of Scandinavia. I didn't know anybody on the coach taking us from Sheffield to London and drifted off to sleep, but Brads and Barnsey soon made their introductions when I woke up!

After being held in a headlock by Barnsey, I couldn't train for two days. And when we played our first game on tour, because of my stiff neck, I couldn't see the crossbar. Every time the ball went over my head, I tipped it over the bar because I couldn't look up. After the game, Harry Bassett said to me, "Can't you catch the ball? What's up with you?"

"I can't f***ing see the crossbar because my neck's still stiff after being attacked!" I replied.

Bassett looked for the right characters to make up his teams and saw the potential in people that others probably didn't. I remember getting on the coach after only a few weeks at the club and Harry said, "Right then, Kelly. You're going to get it."

"What are you on about, Harry?" I replied.

"You're going to get it," he repeated and then started hitting me around the head. I fought back and after a big scuffle he said, "Right, I'll have you next time if you have a bad game." Can you imagine Arsène Wenger saying that to Thierry Henry!?

We had a really tight-knit group and we all used to work together and play together. Derek Dooley, who was the Managing Director and later became chairman, would travel with us. Derek is a lovely fella. As an old pro himself, he used to laugh at the antics we got up to and he'd get involved in the banter, giving as good as he got.

Simon Tracey was the first-choice keeper at United and I was signed because Mel Rees was seriously ill with cancer, although I didn't know that at the time. I didn't meet Mel until we got back from Scandinavia and did pre-season training. We trained at Warminster Road and when I met Mel in the dressing room there, I didn't really know what to say to him. He must have sensed my apprehension because he came up to me and said, "You can shake my hand you know, it's not contagious." The rest of the lads burst out laughing and it really broke the ice.

Mel was an absolute belter of a man and it was an honour to have just had that short time with him. He got back after his initial battle with cancer and was on the bench for a game at Aston Villa. But just a few weeks later, he missed training and we asked the physio, Derek French, why he wasn't there. Frenchy told us that the cancer had returned.

I went to see Mel a week later and he'd lost so much weight. It was such a drastic change and was harrowing to witness. He didn't feel sorry for himself though, he'd laugh and joke about his condition.

I was devastated when Mel died at the obscenely young age of 26.

I made my debut for United early in the 1992/93 season, when I came on as a substitute at Tottenham's White Hart Lane following Simon Tracey's sending off, becoming the first substitute keeper used in the newly created Premier League. I made my full debut in the 1-1 draw at home to Arsenal a few weeks later due to Tracey's suspension. I then got into the side in November after 'Trace' did his shoulder and I finished the season with 43 appearances in all competitions. It was an unbelievable season because we finished in 14th place in the Premier League and reached the semi-finals of the FA Cup, losing to Sheffield Wednesday at Wembley.

When Chris Waddle stepped up to take a free-kick in the opening minutes of that game, as soon as it left his foot, I thought, "I'm in trouble here," and it flew beyond me. After that I had one of those inspired days because everything they hit seemed to hit me. Despite losing 2-1, I enjoyed the game and it was a memorable occasion.

Simon Tracey had been there a few years by the time I signed, so I was initially the understudy. But Tracey then got injured and I did well, so we knew there was competition there. If either of us was out injured for more than two games, the other one generally stayed in the side and in seven years together, I don't think either of us was ever dropped because of a poor performance. There was only a change in goal due to suspension or injury. We had a fantastic goalkeeping coach in Mike Kelly, who's no relation to me. He was the England goalkeeping coach for a long time and was absolutely brilliant. He was the main influence on my career, without a doubt.

Suffering relegation from the Premier League at the end of the 1993/94 season, especially given the circumstances, was a shattering blow. We didn't actually do that bad that season, but it was the number of draws that proved costly. We actually had nine goal-less draws. I thought we defended well, but we just couldn't score the goals.

We beat Newcastle 2-0 in our final home game and I think everybody thought we were safe. Then we went to Oldham in midweek and drew 1-1. We only needed a draw in the last game of the season at Chelsea, I was on the touchline because I wasn't playing. The BBC reporter Ray Stubbs was nearby and he was feeding me the scores from elsewhere. We were 2-1 up and it looked as though we were cruising, but then Chelsea equalised and I remember Wally Downes on the touchline shouting, "You've got to get forward, you've got to score." Right at the end of the match, Glenn Hoddle flicked the ball to Mark Stein, who scored for Chelsea. I was the one who was sent out to check the scores coming in on the TV in the lounge, which was round the corner from the dressing room. Ipswich were playing away at Blackburn and we thought a home win in that game was certain. It was a late result at Ewood Park and they showed the live pictures from there with the Ipswich fans celebrating after a 0-0 result secured their safety. With the other results also going against us, we were down.

On that night's *Match of the Day*, they showed me pushing open the dressing room door and saying, "We're down." There was a sense of utter disbelief because we had appeared to be safe. It's taken the club a long time to recover from that setback.

There was a massive hang-over the following season. If you don't bounce straight back, it can take you two or three years to recover and that proved to be the case. A third keeper, Billy Mercer, was brought in and I had a contractual dispute with Dave Bassett. He dropped me just an hour before kick-off in the game against Notts County at the start of the season, so I found myself out of the side for a short spell. We'd agreed a deal, but it was changed just before I was about to sign the contract before the game. "Let's get on with the football and sort things out after the game," I said. But Harry refused to do that. "No, if you don't sign it now, you're not playing," he said.

Being the pig-headed Irishman that I am, I dug my heels in. "Well, I'm not signing it then," I replied.

After being dropped, I walked out to take my place on the substitutes bench and people were asking me what was happening. "I'll leave Mr Bassett to tell you that," I said. The situation was eventually resolved and I regained my place.

We had a few ding-dongs with Manchester United in the FA Cup around that time. We beat them 2-1 in 1992/93 and then lost 1-0 the following season when Mark Hughes scored. When we drew them for the third year running, I was beaten by a superb chip from Eric Cantona in a 2-0 defeat at Bramall Lane. I was about three or four yards off my line, which is not really considered a long way off, but as soon as he hit it, I remember thinking, "Bloody hell, I'm struggling here."

I was desperately going backwards as the ball hit the underside of the crossbar and went in. It was an unbelievable goal and you just had to applaud it. The funny thing is that I got my studs caught in the netting and couldn't free myself. Someone came to retrieve the ball and left me there, so the referee couldn't re-start the game because I was still stuck in the back of the net!

I was away with the Republic of Ireland squad for a European Championships Play-off game against Holland at Anfield when Harry Bassett left the club in late 1995. Howard Kendall phoned and told me he'd taken over. Howard was brilliant and he transformed things when he took over. He was an incredible man-manager who kept everyone in the squad happy. In his first full season at Bramall Lane, Kendall took us to the Play-off final. I missed it after being injured in the Play-off semi-final second leg at Ipswich. The game was only about five minutes old when I suffered an injury and had my leg strapped up from my ankle to my thigh. With no goalkeeper on the bench, I had to carry on playing. It turned out that I'd ruptured my posterior cruciate ligament, which was quite a serious injury.

Ipswich hit the post at the death before the game went to extra-time. Petr Katchouro and Andy Walker got the goals to send us to the final. My injury was mis-diagnosed, so I was still training up until the day before the final. I remember falling to the ground in agony after trying to kick a ball and the problem was only properly diagnosed in pre-season training, forcing me to miss the start of the new campaign as well.

Nigel Spackman took charge that summer following Kendall's departure to return to his first love, Everton. Coach Willie Donachie used to do a hell of a lot of work on the training pitch and we played some really good football at that time. Greek pair Vas Borbokis and Traianos Dellas came to the club. I got to know Vas and Tri quite well because I regularly used to take them to training, picking them up in Nether Edge on my way in from Derbyshire. Dellas, of course, helped Greece win the 2006 European Championships. He was a huge fella, but he had a great touch. Gordon Cowans was another fantastic player. I rate him as one of the best passers of a ball I've ever seen. We also had my old Republic of Ireland team-mate Paul McGrath, who was at the end of his career. He had the knack of being in the right place at the right time and made things look so easy.

When I reflect on my playing career, the FA Cup quarter-final against Coventry clearly stands out as a memorable match. To make a hat-trick of saves in a tense penalty shoot-out takes some beating, but for it to happen to a proud Irishman on St. Patrick's Day put the icing on the cake.

United were in turmoil in the build-up to the game. We were enjoying a good season under Nigel Spackman up until February/March time, when things seemed to implode. Strike-duo Brian Deane and Jan-Aage Fjortoft were controversially sold on the same day and then Spackman left suddenly, when he realized his squad was being disassembled. It threw everything into chaos, but players just get on with it in a situation like that. You might be shocked for a couple of days, but then you've got to get into the favour of a new manager because that's the nature of the business.

Steve Thompson stepped up from his role on the coaching staff to take charge of the side following Spackman's departure. We lost 1-0 at Ipswich in Thompson's first League game in charge before travelling to Coventry with a place in the FA Cup semi-finals at stake. I was the only survivor from the team who had lost to Sheffield Wednesday in the FA Cup semi-finals five years earlier. Our Brazilian/Portuguese striker Marcelo equalised after Coventry's Dion Dublin had opened the scoring from the penalty spot. Marcelo was a robust centre-forward who did well for us. There was some debate over his nationality. If he had a good game, he was Brazilian; if he had a poor game, he was Portuguese!

The game ended 1-1 after Petr Katchouro wasted a great chance to win it for us. Coventry keeper Steve Ogrizovic came out and kicked the ball against Katchouro, who advanced towards the area. When Petr charged the ball down, he must have had at least four or five yards on Ogrizovic, but he hesitated before shooting. Ogrizovic, who was advanced in years (nearly 40 I think!), sprinted back as if his life depended on it and somehow got his hand to the ball, tipping it away for a corner. I remember seeing Ogrizovic slumped over, clearly thinking, "I never want to have to do that again, running 40 yards."

Defeat would have been very hard on Coventry because we took a bit of a battering in the game and were slightly fortunate to come through it, so we were grateful at having the chance to bring them back to Bramall Lane. I seemed to get a hand to everything they hit that day, prompting Coventry manager Gordon Strachan to describe my performance as 'world-class'.

The battling performance at Coventry persuaded the board to hand the manager's job to Thompson until the end of the season. Dean Saunders was a tremendous mimic and he'd take Thommo off before he came in. Thommo used to say "yeah" when he finished saying something. We would be getting ready for training and Deano would say, "Right, today, I want you all to be at it, yeah?" Then Thommo would come in and say exactly the same thing, having us in stitches, giggling like schoolboys.

Going into the replay against Coventry on the back of a 4-0 win at home over Reading three days earlier, we found ourselves 1-0 down at half-time. Paul Telfer beat me at the Kop end with a long-range free-kick, but he was helped by an uneven patch of turf. The turf, which had been re-laid about a foot outside the six-yard box in the build-up to the game, was left about an inch proud. I remember pointing out the problem to Simon Tracey before the game. "Look at that, if a ball hits that, it's going to fly,'"I said. Sure enough, when Telfer fired in a shot from about 25 or 30 yards out, the ball was going to my right-hand side and, as I went down, it took off after hitting the turf.

Steve Ogrizovic made a great save from centre-half David Holdsworth to protect Coventry's lead and Viorel Moldovan could have put them further ahead when he wasted a free header. It looked as though we were heading for defeat and United fans began streaming out of the ground. But Holdsworth, who had a great game, scored a superb last-minute equaliser to force extra-time. From Roger Nilsen's header, Holdsworth produced what I can only describe as a semi-overhead kick to set it all up for an incredible climax.

We called David 'Reg' (after the Coronation Street character Reg Holdsworth) and he did well for us. He was a very steady player.

We looked the more likely winners in extra-time with Gareth Taylor and Traianos Dellas both going close with headers. But the score remained at 1-1, meaning a penalty shoot-out was required to determine which team went through to the semi-finals. We had been in the same position in 1993, winning a shoot-out against Blackburn at Bramall Lane to set-up that Wembley clash with Wednesday, so I felt confident.

The penalties were taken at the Kop end and we went first. It wasn't a good start for us, however, because striker Gareth Taylor put his effort straight at Steve Ogrizovic. Gareth was absolutely distraught and I remember him walking back and saying to me, "Come on, Ned. I need you to get me out of this now." Gareth and I are actually good mates and I'm godfather to his kids.

Dion Dublin then stepped up. He had a reputation as a player who never missed penalties and had also put a penalty past me in the first game. I've always had a theory that most penalty-takers, if they score, will continue to put the ball the same side because they'll bet on themselves to beat the keeper, even if he goes early. As soon as Dublin walked up, I thought, "I'm going to save this, no problem." I thought I'd go so early that I could almost have a cigarette by the time he hit it! It was such a simple save because I went that early. I was laughing to myself because it was such a great feeling to have guessed right. I've got a picture at home, which shows that just as Dublin is about to strike the ball, I'm diving already.

With the tension mounting, it was then the turn of Norwegian defender Roger Nilsen. He never scored a goal for United from open play, but he could really strike a ball. Roger was unlucky because his shots always seemed to skim a post or just go over the bar. That was not the case on this occasion, however, as he fired home to put us ahead 1-0.

David Burrows took Coventry's second penalty. He had a helluva left foot and just used to absolutely cane the ball as hard as he could. I decided that I would half-dive and half-stand-up. So, when he took the penalty, I partially dived to my left, threw my hand back and the ball smacked against my wrist, nearly breaking it. The ball got a reverse spin, hit the far post and fortunately stayed out.

After making two penalty saves, I was thinking to myself what a night it was turning out to be!

Petr Katchouro could have eased the tension for us by putting away our third penalty, but he put his effort well off-target. Petr was always a very confident striker of a ball, but he just didn't get it right that time and I was thinking, "Here we go again."

Paul Telfer was Coventry's third penalty-taker and he was another lad who had a great shot. I got my fingers to the ball, but there was so much power in the strike that it knocked my middle and index fingers back and they were black and blue the following day. I was glad I didn't get a full hand on the ball because I don't think I'd have found it again! That made it 1-1 after three penalties each.

After Bobby Ford put his penalty away to put us 2-1 up, I faced their centre-forward, Welshman Simon Haworth. As he walked towards me, I remember thinking to myself, "No, he's not going to score, this lad." As a goalkeeper, you usually pick a side and go that way, but I wasn't sure he knew where he was going to put it, so I decided to half stand up to him. Sure enough, Haworth put a weak penalty to my right and I stopped it easily: a goalkeeper's hat-trick on 'Paddy's Night' – it doesn't get any better than that. Talk about being pumped up; I thought the veins in my neck were going to burst.

Knowing that a successfully taken penalty would give us victory, Wayne Quinn stepped up and hammered the ball home. His left foot strike went across Ogrizovic, into the top corner of the net. I think Wayne had it in his mind that even if Ogrizovic went the right way, he still wouldn't get it.

It was bedlam after that with fans swarming onto the pitch to celebrate. I was lifted up and one or two lads decided to take my boots off. I used to have them tied on tightly and I could feel that my ankle bone was about to dislocate, so I had to punch the lad who was pulling the boot. "Oi, my bloody ankle's about to pop out!" I shouted. After he apologised, I said that if he wanted them he could have them, so I unlaced my boots and handed them to him. It seemed to take about half an hour to get off the pitch.

Simon Tracey was one of the first to come up and congratulate me, which illustrates the relationship we had, despite being rivals for the goal-keeper's jersey. If he did well, I was the first to say, "Well done" to him and vice-versa.

It was a relief that the freak first-half goal I had conceded didn't prove to be crucial. When I saw groundsman Kelly Barrowclough at the end of the game, I joked, "That bloody pitch!"

When we came to play the next home game, he'd had the pitch shaved right down. "You're not blaming me this time!" he said.

The euphoria of winning a penalty shoot-out is captured in a series of three photos I have at home, showing my celebrations after each save. There's elation etched on my face. I was in the mood for a celebratory drink after the match, but that idea was a non-starter. It may have been St. Patrick's Day, but the game had gone on that long all the bloody pubs had shut, so I couldn't get a pint! I ended up having a cup of tea instead and going to bed.

We faced Newcastle at Old Trafford in the semi-finals of the Cup. Thommo's closing gee-up to the lads two minutes before we went out was caught on camera and I had to laugh when I later saw it on TV. "Aye lads, yeah. You're ninety f***ing minutes away from immor-f***ing-tality!" Sadly, there was to be no repeat of the quarter-final drama because it was a nothing game. It always seemed likely that someone was going to win by a goal and that's how it turned out. Unfortunately, it was Newcastle who won it, following a goal from Alan Shearer. Wayne Quinn had our only real chance with a shot which Shay Given turned round the post.

There was further disappointment at the end of the season when we were beaten by Sunderland in the semi-finals of the Play-offs. Thommo was shown on TV at the end of the second leg with his head in his hands and I think he realised then that his chances of landing the manager's job permanently had disappeared. I wasn't in the side for the game at Sunderland, so I was involved in Hallam FM's commentary and had to interview Thommo live on the radio at the end of the game, which was quite bizarre.

I left United in the summer of 1999 when Adrian Heath took over as manager. We'd gone up to St. Andrews in Scotland during pre-season and I think Aberdeen were trying to buy me at the time. To be honest, I didn't want to leave, but I was effectively told by Heath that I was going. "You're nearly 31 and you've got a year left on your contract, so we're going to sell you," he said. Blackburn came in for me, offered the money United wanted and gave me a four-year contract. My last game for United was in a pre-season friendly against Chelsea and we lost 2-0. When I waved to the fans at the end of the game, I think they knew and I knew that it was the end of my seven-year spell with this great club. I'd had a fantastic time at Bramall Lane, so I was very sad to go.

I was forced to retire from playing in 2004 following a freak training ground injury. I was training with some of the Blackburn academy lads, showing them what to do and when one of them hit a ball too early, I instinctively went after it. My finger hit the turf, 14 stone landed on top of it and completely shattered it. I lost my grip in the finger and for a keeper that's obviously a problem. I think I'd had my time by then, with every part of my body calling "Stop" after nearly 20 years. I can't complain because I had a great career.

I became the Republic of Ireland goalkeeping coach when Steve Staunton was appointed manager in 2005 and I'm really enjoying the role. One of the keepers I work with is Paddy Kenny and I've been really impressed with him. United have another good keeper there.

In the two years between the end of my playing career and joining the Republic of Ireland set-up, I had a break from football. That allowed me to get involved in a commercial property company with a business partner and I've found it fascinating.

I still see some of my old team-mates from time to time. I've been with Simon Tracey on an FA goalkeeper coaching course in Wales and I also met up with a number of my old team-mates at Mick Rooker's 50th birthday party. Mick is the Promotions Manager at Bramall Lane and does a lot of work behind the scenes. Paul Beesley, John Gannon, Carl Bradshaw and Dane Whitehouse were among those who attended and we had an fantastic night. The Blades fans are fantastic and they always give me a tremendous reception when I visit the club. United's return to the Premiership is long overdue and I'm delighted to see them there.

PHIL JAGIELKA
MIDFIELDER 1999–PRESENT

BORN   17 August 1982, Manchester
SIGNED   August 1999 from Apprentice
BLADES CAREER   249 games, 18 goals
HONOURS   Promotion from Championship 2005/06, 6 England
Under-21 caps

* statistics correct to 1 August 2006

A versatile player who is equally at home in midfield or defence, Phil has
also performed admirably on several occasions as an emergency goalkeeper.
Jagielka was an influential figure as United made their long-awaited return
to the Premiership in 2006, winning the Player of the Year award. He
pledged his future to the club at the beginning of the 2006/07 season,
signing a new three-year contract.

Sheffield United 3 v Hull City 2

The Championship
Saturday 8 April 2006

Bramall Lane
Attendance: 26,324

Relief all round as Unsworth smashes a last-minute winner, following a
Hull comeback, to put the Blades on the brink of promotion

Teams

Neil Warnock	**Managers**	Peter Taylor
Paddy Kenny		Boaz Myhill
Rob Kozluk		Alton Thelwell
David Unsworth		Leon Cort
Craig Short		Damien Delaney
Chris Morgan		Andrew Dawson
Phil Jagielka		Keith Andrews
Paul Ifill		Billy Paynter
(Sub. Steve Kabba)		(Sub. Stuart Elliott)
Michael Tonge		Stuart Green
Chris Armstrong		Kevin Ellison
Neil Shipperley		Craig Fagan
		(Sub. Darryl Duffy)
Danny Webber		Jon Parkin
Shipperley 36, Ifill 52	**Scorers**	Elliott 65, Duffy 70
Unsworth 90		

Referee: P Crossley

WHEN DAVID UNSWORTH scored at the death to give us victory over Hull, I felt a burst of happiness coupled with the relief of not having thrown the game away. Hull had come back from 2-0 down to level before Unsworth struck deep into injury time. The whole stadium erupted and you sort of half knew then that we'd done it. You were thinking, 'This MUST be the season now.' If we'd have drawn, the feeling would have been that we still weren't quite there yet. And we were all fed up with the creeping run of results which endangered promotion to the Premier League.

The Hull game would have been a fitting way to end the season, but we had to settle for the fact that we were nearly there. After we won at Cardiff the following Friday, promotion was confirmed when Leeds were held to a draw at home to Reading a day later, sparking a whole series of celebrations.

I started out as a kid playing for a team called Sale United, based in the area I come from in Manchester. After we faced Stone Dominoes in a friendly, I went down to Staffordshire on a trial basis and ended up playing for them for a couple of seasons. Stone Dominoes was a little feeder club for Stoke City before the Acadamies started. The coach who had mentored me at Stone left to go and coach at Everton and I followed him a year later. I was quite comfortable with how things went and what was happening at Goodison, but they weren't prepared to offer me more than a 12-month contract, which I decided to turn down.

I lost a bit of self-confidence and went on trial to Manchester City, where I was absolutely rubbish. I then came to Sheffield United for a week with another player who'd been at Everton, who was my best mate from where I lived. It was down to the Howard Kendall connection. He'd gone back to manage Everton from United. 'Mad Monty' (Nick Montgomery) was also on trial at the same time as us two. I trained with the YTS players for a week, played in a few games and did okay, prompting coaches Russell Slade and Steve Myles to offer me a scholarship.

I was training with the first-team at the age of 17 and appeared as a substitute against Swindon in the last game of the 1999/2000 season. The following season was quite frustrating because people like Monty and

Michael Tonge came through and they sort of overtook me. I would train every day of the week, play a reserve match and then train with the first-team instead of going to college, so I didn't have any days off. It made it a long week and I took a backward step, whereas Monty and Tongey pushed through. I did have a good run in the first team in the second-half of the 2001/02 season and then my career sort of kicked on from there.

The 2002/03 campaign was, of course, the 'nearly' season, when we reached the Play-off final and the semi-finals of both Cup competitions. I'll always remember scoring from distance against Leeds in the Worthington Cup. I doubt that I'll ever hit the target from that distance again, never mind put it where I did. You look back at moments in your career and obviously that's going to be one of the major highlights. There was a picture done of my goal and I was given the first copy to be printed off. It's one of my most prized possessions.

The FA Cup semi-final against Arsenal summed up the whole season. 'Chief' (Wayne Allison) got fouled, referee Graham Poll ended up half-tackling Tongey and I actually thought I was going to get a block on Freddy Ljungberg's shot, but it somehow went in. Then there was David Seaman's save from Paul Peschisolido's header from nanometers out and I had a decent follow-up chance, but it was never meant to be our day.

Then of course there was the Play-off final against Wolves, when you just wanted to walk off with about 20 or 30 minutes left. If we'd have got a goal back, we'd have been in there, but they were so comfortable. We hit a post, missed a penalty and never had a chance to put a little bit of pressure on them. I'll never forget the sight of Wolves owner Sir Jack Hayward, shown on the big screen, celebrating with about five minutes to go. Losing that match brought the two semi-final defeats back. If we'd won that match, we'd have said it was the best season ever and that we were unlucky in the two semi-finals. But in the three chances we had to do something decent, we didn't do anything. To get to two semi-finals and the Play-off final in the same season was frightening. I'll never forget what Wayne Allison said to me. 'You might never have as good a season as this,' he told me. I was thinking, 'Hang on, this is my first full season.'

The following season was a strange one. After doing so well the previous season, we were fancied to go straight up. But a few players came and went and it just never really worked out. We weren't doing anything particularly different, but we weren't making the comebacks in games that we'd done previously. Michael Brown, who'd scored 22 goals the season before, missed the start of the season and was then sold to Spurs in January. We improved in the 2004/05 season and still had a chance of making the Play-offs in the last game, but that didn't happen either.

We went to China in preparation for the 2005/06 campaign and had to deal with problems like jet-lag after ten flights in ten days, so we were a bit cautious as to whether that would take it out of us come Christmas. If we had a three-hour flight, it was another two-hour bus journey afterwards, so it wasn't as well planned as it could have been. We were going to travel to China again this summer, but the World Cup put a stop to those plans. If we had done, we'd have flown to one place and spent ten days there, with different teams flown in to play us, rather than do a tour of China.

After Wigan came in for me and made it public how much they thought I was worth, it put a little bit of pressure on my performances, with people thinking I was worth so much money. Some clubs would keep you in the dark and not let you know anything about interest like that, but I was told by the Gaffer exactly what was happening. We often chatted and I'm sure that if I'd struggled to cope with everything, he would have been there to help me. Because I knew where I stood and nothing really came of it, it made life easier for me. The worse thing you want to do is pick up a paper and think, "Hang on, what's going on here?" As long as you get things straight out in the open, then everything is easily sorted out within five minutes, rather than keeping it quiet for a couple of weeks. It's just a better way to do things. If I'd have said to the Gaffer that I wanted to go, I'm sure that he'd have agreed, so long as it was a decent enough offer for the club. But, as it was, he rang me, told me that United didn't want to sell and I was more than happy to stay. In previous years, I'd have been gone and probably half the money, or even just a quarter of it, would have been spent in the transfer market. Two years earlier, even, they'd have perhaps taken half the amount that was offered for me, so that was another sign that the club was progressing.

It wasn't so much said, but you could just sense that we were going to take it by the scruff of the neck and have a decent go in 2005/06. Neil Warnock had only one season left on his contract and he was desperate to give it a big go because he knew it was going to be his final chance to take us up. He was a little bit frustrated in his first few years at the club because he didn't have much money, but then he was able to bring in players like Paul Ifill and Danny Webber. Andy Gray's transfer gave him some more money to spend and we ended up getting in some decent loan signings as well, so it all sort of fell into place. The Gaffer is quite shrewd, signing players whose careers are maybe going the wrong way and managing to turn them round. He's done that with a lot of players, getting them in for not a lot of money and making them a little bit special. The team-spirit we've got is down to the players he's brought in. When there's a choice between two players and one may be better than the other, but might cause a bit of disturbance to the squad, the Gaffer would rather go for the team player and take more of a gamble. He's had a number of promotions and he knows what it's all about.

We had a good, if slightly fortunate, start to the season. Our opening game against Leicester was live on Sky TV and we had a little bit of luck with a penalty decision, ending up winning 4-1. It looked fantastic on paper, but the score-line flattered us. From there, we had the best start since I've been at the club. We won our first two, lost at QPR and then won seven on the spin, so confidence was sky-high and we had a couple of points to play with if we did have a dip. We've normally had to catch up since I've been in the team, finding ourselves six or seven points behind after four or five games, so getting points on the board helped us out massively. It's all about picking up the momentum.

David Unsworth arrived at the club in the opening weeks of the season, joining other experienced signings like Neil Shipperley and Keith Gillespie. We didn't have that sort of experience the season before. I think Andy Liddell and Chris Morgan, at 30 and 27 respectively, were the oldest players in the side at that time. In this campaign, we had a few players who'd played 300 games plus and when the going got tough or we were having a bad half an hour, they knew what to do and how to express themselves. When things don't go well and chances are being missed, young players can sometimes go into their shell. 'Unsy' has played in the Premiership for so many years. He may have lost a yard of pace because he's a bit older, but his distribution is fantastic.

'Shipps' was just a focal point up front for us to play off and it's nice to know what you're going to get from someone like him. Obviously he's got his limitations; he's probably lost a yard of pace in recent years, but he's probably gained that in his head because he's got so much experience. Having Keith Gillespie in the squad also made a big difference because he's a fantastic footballer. He would come on and give us a different option. Paul Ifill is a bit more direct than Keith, getting the ball and running at people, whereas when Keith gets it, you know a cross is going to come in and you can time your run to try to meet it.

It worked so well for us with Nick Montgomery playing alongside me in midfield. Having played in defence, a lot of people assumed I'd want to play the holding role in midfield. We worked well as a partnership, with him in the holding role, allowing me to get forward. I scored more goals than I've ever scored before. I know more or less everything about Monty and I'm sure he'd say exactly the same. We don't even need to tell each other what is happening; it just sort of happens naturally. I know when he's going to go on a dribble, just by the way he goes and gets the ball. It's so much better when you're working as a partnership in there because someone needs to sit in when the other one goes forward.

Steven Kabba enjoyed a great start to the season after a terrible time with injuries. He had tendonitis in his knee, a broken leg and an Achilles problem – all in the space of about 18 months. I don't know how he managed to cope during that period because if I have a couple of days on the treatment table, I'm ready for off. It's easy to forget how well 'Kabbs' did because it was the early part of the season, but if you look at the DVD, he was absolutely on fire. It was frightening how well he started. Danny Webber got injured in the warm-up for the home game against Coventry, giving Kabbs a chance. He scored and never looked back. 'Webbs' and Kabbs are the type you can give the ball to and know they'll create something out of nothing, which was something we'd not had for a few seasons.

The Gaffer changed things round a little bit for the game at Millwall in October with Tongey coming in. The New Den's not a nice place to go to, so to come away with a 4-0 win was fantastic, no matter how much they were struggling at the time. I think people expected us to go on a big dip at some point, but that result set down a bit of a marker. We had to deal with uncertainty surrounding the Gaffer's future in November. You could understand why he was definitely thinking about it when Portsmouth came in for him after their manager Alain Perrin was sacked. My dream was to play in the Premiership and I'm sure his dream was to manage in the Premiership. Added to that, the Board weren't too forthcoming in offering him a new contract, with his existing one so close to expiring, so he was put in a difficult situation. With us seriously challenging for promotion, the last thing we all needed was a disturbance. You never know, someone could have come in as the new manager if the Gaffer had left, and we could have still been promoted. But someone could have come in who wanted to do it their way – just to prove they had got us promoted instead of the Gaffer – and then disrupted things. When it's not broken, you don't want it to be fixed. We were desperate for the Gaffer to stay and thankfully he did.

Neil Warnock has had a massive influence on my career. I know he wasn't the person who brought me to the club, but I've got a lot to thank him for because I've played nearly 250 games and I've just turned 24. Kevin Blackwell also had a massive influence, especially on the young lads. He was fantastic and his training sessions were brilliant. Sometimes when he'd been quite harsh with you in training, he'd pull you and ask how you felt about that. I'd say, "To be honest Blackie, if you're being harsh on me because you don't like me, then obviously I'm not going to be happy. But if you're being harsh because you want me to be as good as I can be, then I'm more than happy for you to do that." David Kelly, who'd played for United, came back as Blackwell's replacement and he had a slightly different way of doing things. He was a bit more relaxed and there was a lot more fun, so it was good in a different way. I was a little bit disappointed when he left to become Preston's assistant-manager, but it was a good opportunity for him. Sometimes the Gaffer only allows his assistant to have so much input because he's got his own ways of doing things and with the age difference between him and the Gaffer, Ned's ways were sometimes more different than anyone else. Stuart McCall stepped up to the plate following Ned's departure and he's doing a fantastic job. His enthusiasm is amazing and I think he still wants to be training himself. He's learning and getting more experience week by week. If you look at his football CV, every box is ticked and I'm sure he's looking to do the same either as a coach or manager at the top level.

We went out at the third round stage in both the FA Cup and Carling Cup. Normally, we'd look to go as far as we can in the Cups and be really disappointed when we lose, but the attitude that season was that it was a promotion campaign. We thought, "Anything else that comes is a bonus, but we're not too fussed."

We had the odd setback along the way, of course. I scored in the game at home to Norwich on Boxing Day to put us 1-0 up, but then it all went massively pear-shaped. We just went a little bit flat and ended up losing 3-1. We also crashed to a 4-1 defeat at home to Watford in February live on Sky TV. They did really well and before you knew it, we were 3-0 down. Unsy got sent off following a forearm smash on Chris Eagles, our defence had a bit of an off-day and Marlon King was on fire.

The Gaffer brought in the likes of Ade Akinbiyi, Garry Flitcroft and Chris Lucketti to add a bit of depth to the squad, so that if anything did go wrong, we had some experience there. Watford and Leeds were starting to put pressure on us. That's when it kicked in and we thought, "Hang on, we better pull our fingers out a little bit." If it had all gone pear-shaped following a couple of bad results, after being in second place all season, it would have been devastating. The chasing teams have got nothing to lose if they keep going and going with something to chase. Reading had gone a bit too far ahead of us and they didn't really need to look down because they were so far ahead of third. When we drew, Reading won and as soon as they got close to double figures ahead, you started looking at the teams below, knowing we were defending the second promotion place. With the connections some of our squad have with Crystal Palace, particularly Shipps and Kabbs, one or two of their players were saying they were going to catch us. Shipps was texting Michael Hughes, saying, "We're not worried about you, mate" and things like that.

We were a bit all over the shop in the game at Coventry, losing 2-0. We then lost 2-1 at Norwich, but we gained a lot more confidence from that game because we didn't think we should have lost. Basically, we were rubbish at Coventry, but we were back to somewhere near where we should have been at Norwich. After beating Southampton 3-0, Webbs got us out of the mire at Stoke, scoring to earn a draw, after a pathetic performance. Crystal Palace then lost at Leicester in midweek, which more or less killed-off their chances.

The other chasing teams had messed up a bit as well, so the finishing line was in sight as we prepared for the visit of Hull. Hull started brightly with Keith Andrews going close. Paddy Kenny also made a good save to keep out an effort from Kevin Ellison, but Shipps settled our nerves when he scored after getting on the end of a cross from Tongey. Shipps was an absolute rock for us, playing in most of the games and scoring some important goals. A lot of fans were surprised that he'd scored so many goals, but none of the boys were surprised after training with him and getting to know how he played. People pick Shipps up on his size, but he's just a physically big person. He could not eat for three years and still not be any smaller! His game's not all about headers and roughing up defenders, though; he's got great technique and it worked wonders for us.

It was good to see Tongey come back and do well after struggling with his form at the start of the season. Because he was on the left, I think he was relying on people to give him the ball. If he didn't receive it, there wasn't much he could do to affect the game. That meant that when he did get hold of it, he tried to affect the play too much and probably sometimes played balls which were too difficult. Once a few of those go missing, your confidence plummets and I think that's what happened to Mike. Unfortunately, he was a bit-part player in the first-half of the season, but it made him mature massively and he was our best player by far in the second-half of the season. I room with Mike, so we had a lot of chats and we knew he had to go back in the middle to get his confidence back. After doing that, I think he proved to everyone what a fantastic player he is.

Hull keeper Boaz Myhill turned an effort from Danny Webber over the bar before Webbs supplied a cross for Paul Ifill to score with his head. 'Ifes' did the baby celebration after scoring that goal, following the birth of his baby girl and we thought we were home and dry. 2-0 up with less than half an hour to go. But a double substitution sparked a Hull revival, with Stuart Elliott and Darryl Duffy both finding the net midway through the second-half after coming on.

Elliott scored at the far post after getting on the end of a cross from Alton Thelwell. In the build-up to the goal, Paddy got kicked in the head, which I think was by one of our players. He came out for the ball, there was a scramble and he ended up being half knocked-out. You looked at Paddy and you could tell he wasn't totally there. I thought that if he wasn't going to be right, he should come off to prevent doing any more damage, so that he'd be OK for the rest of the season. Knowing very well that we'd not got a keeper on the bench, I knew that I would be called on to go in nets if he was substituted. I untucked my shirt, ready to swap it with Paddy, but he's a tough character and he insisted he was okay to carry on. "No, no, I'll be all right, I'll be all right," he said. But I could tell he wasn't OK, because he wasn't even looking at me properly when he said that because he was so far gone.

I'd acted as a stand-in keeper previously after messing about in goal on the training ground. The keepers have a shooting game between themselves and I joined in a couple of times as keeper for them. I enjoyed it and things progressed from there. Paddy got injured down at Crystal Palace and Pesch wanted to take over because he loves going in goal. But the Gaffer looked at his short stature and realised that he wanted someone else, so I went in nets. I thought I'd enjoy it more than I did. I was so, so nervous. They were coming over the half-way line and I was bravely thinking, "Come on, have a shot, have a shot." But, as they got closer to the goal, I was now thinking, "Oh God, please clear it, please clear it." It was so nerve-wracking because you don't mind if someone has a shot and it goes straight into the top corner; it's the ones you're expected to save that are a worry – you're scared that the ball will bobble and go through your legs.

Once the Palace game was over, I felt such a buzz and I got Paddy to give me the shirt that I wore.

Hull were lifted by the goal and, with Paddy struggling, it was an anxious spell for us. Morgs ran into Paddy during a mix-up over a ball played into the area and I was thinking, "Shit, what's going on now?" Then we had a let-off when the referee decided against awarding a penalty after Paddy grabbed Green's leg inside the area and brought him down. But then, five minutes after Hull had pulled a goal back, Duffy struck the equaliser to set up a tense finish.

Fortunately, after looking as though he would be forced to go off, Paddy managed to get it together and looked as though he'd come round. There weren't any real chances at either end until, with the match going into stoppage time, Kabbs had an effort turned off-target by Myhill. The resulting corner was on the right and Unsy normally takes them from that side, but for some reason we decided to go for an out-swinger, so he took up a position inside the box. When the corner came over, Craig Short headed the ball down, Webber had a shot saved and Unsy was there to smash the ball home with his left foot. It was a fantastic moment as we celebrated the goal. I'm surprised Unsy's alive because everyone jumped on top of him, whacking him in the face and all sorts; it's amazing he could breathe! Every single person was so, so happy; they were like ten-year-old kids who'd won the FA Cup Final. For someone who's been there and done it over the years, it was great to see that Unsy was just as excited as all the young lads.

We knew that a win at Cardiff on the Friday would give us a chance of going up that weekend. In a dire game, another Sky TV match, Webbs scored a great goal, curling the ball round the keeper. We half-celebrated at the end of the match because we were so many points clear. We all decided to meet up the next day at the training ground to watch the results coming in, with a lot of champagne on hand. If Leeds failed to win at home to Reading, we were up. Unsy had come over from Liverpool and Webbs had come from Manchester, while Kabbs came all the way back from London after seeing his family. It was 1-0 to Leeds, with about half an hour left, so we were thinking it could turn out to be an anti-climax. But then good old Hunt scored for Reading and the whole place erupted. The champagne was flowing and Morgs and I ended up going to a radio station half-drunk, speaking to fans who phoned up. We all went out for a drink later, which is a bit of a blur.

It was strange because we'd celebrated at Cardiff, then after the Leeds game because it was the first time we could celebrate in front of the fans. That was followed by the last game of the season against Crystal Palace, when we received the plaque and did a lap of honour. We also had the Player of the Year dinner and then an open-top bus trip to a civic reception at the Town Hall. These are memories you'll always remember. It was mad and you sort of got sick of celebrating by the end! We did about three weeks of celebrating and it all got a bit too much.

I signed a new three-year contract at the start of this season and hopefully I'll have the whole three years at the club and then be close to a testimonial. If we weren't spending any money and everything was a joke, I wouldn't have been so quick to sign a new contract. But the club has changed so much in the six years I've been here. When I first came to the club, we rented a training pitch at Millhouses. We used to change in the away dressing room at Bramall Lane and travel up in an old mini-bus. You compare that to what we've got now at the Academy, with superb facilities and a number of pitches to choose from. The stadium also looks so much better with the corner stand in there. Everything is in place and now we have to try and remain in the Premiership and make the most of it. I think the club has a bright future and I want to be part of that and make as many appearances as I can.

I started the season in midfield and I see myself as a midfielder, but I don't know what the Gaffer thinks! I think my versatility helped me to get into the team to begin with. If I was on the bench, it helped that I could play in a couple of positions. As it is now, I wouldn't say it's becoming a pain, but it's hard to sort of master one position when you only play there for two or three weeks. It's hard to jump straight from midfield to playing at the back and play as well as you possibly can. You can't just do it overnight; sometimes it works and sometimes it doesn't. It helps if you train all week in a position, but if someone gets an injury on a Friday and there's no-one else to cover, you're thrown in at the deep end. I don't mind doing it for the team, but it's frustrating sometimes. Last season was OK because I played most of my games in midfield, although some people still tell me I'm probably more suited to playing in defence, at right-back or centre-back. I'm not really sure what my best position is myself, but I'd like to give it a crack in midfield.

In terms of midfielders in this country, you can't look any further than Steven Gerrard from my point of view. He's definitely the man and it was a strange feeling playing against him on the opening day of the season. In the Premiership, you find yourself playing against Gerrard and then, four days later, you're facing Edgar Davids. It carries on and on and on like that. You can't think too much about one particular player or one particular team because once that game is over, there's another game round the corner, against a team containing a number of fully fledged internationals. That's what makes the Premiership so exciting. The whole experience is fantastic, playing at some great stadiums, and it's just a case of whether we can cut it.

We're realistic, the main aim is survival and that's the same for any team coming up to the Premiership. If we stay up, I don't think we'll be the bookies favourites to go down the following season. Hopefully we'll stay up this season and build on it from there.